THE F-FRAME MOULTONS

by Tony Hadland

LIT

Bibliographic information published by the Deutsche Nationalbibliothek
The Deutsche Nationalbibliothek lists this publication in the Deutsche Nationalbibliografie; detailed bibliographic data are available on the Internet at http://dnb.d-nb.de.

ISBN 978-3-643-90830-8

A catalogue record for this book is available from the British Library

Klosbachstr. 107
CH-8032 Zürich
Tel. +41 (0) 44-251 75 05
E-Mail: zuerich@lit-verlag.ch http://www.lit-verlag.ch
Distribution:
In the UK: Global Book Marketing, e-mail: mo@centralbooks.com
In North America: International Specialized Book Services, e-mail: orders@isbs.com
In Germany: LIT Verlag Fresnostr. 2, D-48159 Münster
Tel. +49 (0) 2 51-620 32 22, Fax +49 (0) 2 51-922 60 99, e-mail: vertrieb@lit-verlag.de
In Austria: Medienlogistik Pichler-ÖBZ, e-mail: mlo@medien-logistik.at
e-books are available at www.litwebshop.de

To Rosemary,
without whose patience and support this
book would not have been written.

Tony Hadland on the 1988 North of Scotland Moulton tour with a modified 1965 Moulton Deluxe

CONTENTS

N.B. Each Chapter is relatively self-contained and hence the book is especially suitable for "dipping into" with a minimum of cross reference. An Additional Reading List is provided at the end of each Chapter.

Dr. Alex Moulton, C.B.E., R.D.I.

FOREWORD

My intention in the creation of the Moulton bicycle was to take the evolution of that most remarkable device a stage beyond its classical form. In other words to produce a bicycle which was more pleasing to have and to use.

To get this endeavour into reality involved the labour of many devoted people, some of whom are with me still. The painstaking research done nearly a generation later by Tony Hadland, which has resulted in this book, is I regard a tribute to them without whom my concept would not have been realised.

One of the most pleasing consequences of the Moulton Bicycle epic so far has been the spontaneous growth of the Moulton Users' groups: and to meet and to ride with them gives me special pleasure. To them I commend this book as a unique source of detailed information to help them derive enjoyment from the use of their old machines.

For myself, reading the narrative has put my present further intentions into perspective as a continuing link of the evolutionary process I started in the 1950's.

Dr. Alex Moulton, C.B.E.
The Hall,
Bradford on Avon

This Book in Context, a Third of a Century On

It is an oft-heard statement that, when Tony Hadland first suggested to me that I write a book about Moultons, I bounced the idea back to him, as I was "too busy". In fact, Tony and I had been in correspondence with regard to his Moulton interest and I had been most impressed, both with his eloquent writing skills and his knowledge. He was, to my mind, the ideal man for the job.

I could, perhaps, have been forgiven for being "too busy". It was in the spring of 1980.

Mark Ottaway had just devoted half a page in *The Sunday Times* to the activities of Moulton Preservation, which I had recently started, born from indignation at the reigning attitude in most cycle shops and more generally, that the Moulton was to be avoided. It was "dangerous", one "had to pedal too much", it was "a joke" – and, as far as I was concerned, worst of all, it was "different". In my view, now well accepted, it was a superior concept, elegantly conceived but badly executed by its builders of the time, and badly maintained by hostile cycle establishments.

I knew *nothing* about cycle maintenance or engineering but, recognising just how beautiful and *better* the Moulton was in comparison with other bikes, I felt that this endangered species was in urgent need of preservation.

Mark had warned me that a few letters might arrive as a result of his article. In fact, over fifty appeared in the next post! Clearly, I was not alone in my sentiments. And that is why I was "too busy"! My two rooms were filled with discarded Moultons that *Sunday Times* readers donated from their sheds, and those bikes that were too wrecked became donors to those that were in need. Some readers came forward with skills that could provide much-needed rare parts and somehow, organically, Moulton Preservation grew to ensure a future for the F-frame Moultons.

Of course they were not then known as F-frames, for there *was* no Spaceframe Moulton.

In 1980, when this book was first considered, it was 6 years since Raleigh had produced the last Mk3. Original spares from Moulton Developments at The Hall were in extremely short supply and Alex Moulton was only considering whether to press ahead commercially and independently with the AM project. The publicity generated both by Moulton Preservation and this book meant that, by 1981, the traditional September gathering of the Moulton Bicycle Club at The Hall, Bradford on Avon swelled from a dozen or so to several hundred attendees. This renewed enthusiasm heartened and strengthened Alex Moulton's resolve to go ahead independently with the launch of the AM project.

That was the scene into which Tony and I entered when the seeds of both the Preservation plan and the book were first planted. What allowed those seeds to germinate was the incredible input of wisdom and goodwill from the enlightened minority in the cycling world who had vision enough to recognise the Moulton as a bicycle "more pleasing to have and to use" – in the words of its remarkable creator.

Whilst historically, the "Blue Book" was born from a time when the Moulton was in relative obscurity, we must now ask what relevance it has today, in another century, when the Moulton Bicycle is revered as a design icon.

This book remains central to Moultoneering, both as an icon in itself, and as the first 'touchstone' that aspiring "Moultoneers" were, and can still be guided by.

Since its first publication, fine works such as Paul Grogan's *Classic Moulton* books have come along, giving attractive and detailed insights into the Moulton world, but Tony's book remains a classic in its own right and a "must-have" for every Moultoneer's bookshelf. So what has changed since this book instigated the revival of the Moulton bicycle, its recognition as a milestone in cycle design and its "call to arms" to Moulton cyclists as one body – the "Moultoneers"?

The first major development must have been the coming of the Spaceframe. This neatly skirted round the Raleigh-held patents as a completely different creation. It could not be known as a Moulton (the name being owned by Raleigh after they bought the concern in 1967) and so it became known as the "Alex Moulton" or "AM". It gave Alex the chance freely to pursue the ultimate in his quest for the perfect cycle, with no restrictions. Lightweight aircraft tubing, interlaced, intricate geometric formations gave a rigidity of frame, coupled with superior suspension – qualities that created one of the lightest, fastest, human-powered machines of its time.

Whereas the F-frame was initially painted in billiard cue style, in an attempt to visually shorten the long vertical tubes for aesthetic reasons, at a time when the Moulton's appearance visually challenged conventional cycle design, the AM was altogether less compromising. At first glance, when launched in 1983, it appeared as a floating filigree pattern; a miniature Forth Bridge or the Meccano set of a child genius! In its austere dark grey, it made no effort to be pretty – yet there was an inherent stylishness in its pure functionality. This was more accentuated in the later, stainless, "pylon" space frames. But in its quest for perfection, some might say that the AM became too rarefied. Brilliant as it was, you couldn't lock it outside the supermarket.

A bicycle is, at its heart, a humble, functional object. The brilliance of the F-frame was that its arrival shot cycle design forward, yet it retained its utilitarian function perfectly. It was able to stun, surprise, speed and sparkle – or slog home with the shopping! The Spaceframe reached for the skies – but it cost the earth! However, in 1988, responding to the growing interest in off-road cycling, Alex launched the All Terrain Bicycle – the 20" wheel ATB – a gutsy Spaceframe that later evolved into the APB (All purpose Bicycle). Produced by Pashley Cycles at Stratford-upon-Avon (coincidentally Alex Moulton's birthplace on another River Avon) the APB was an affordable alternative to the AM range and continues in Pashley production as the TSR range, continually refined under the design skills of Dan Farrell, and serving as a good "entry model" Moulton, as well as being a solid, practical bike.

So the Spaceframe, in its lightweight, separable, speedy or affordable forms, has indeed achieved its own greatness, lauded by designers, architects and engineers, world-wide. Initially, Alex's delight and preoccupation with the Spaceframe led him to refer to the F-frame as "that dead bike", but F-frames were developing a growing, loyal following, increasingly seen as an "iconic" design. They remained true to themselves and carried that beauty that is often inherent at the inception of a revolutionary creation.

Therefore it was with huge pleasure that we greeted the return of the F-frame in the form of the Bridgestone Moulton, soon after the turn of this century. The Bridgestone was the result of Alex's careful revisiting of F-frame design, going "back to basics" in his characteristic manner. It was immediately clear that Alex had radically revisited every aspect of the F-frame and addressed any points of potential improvement. The ability to detach from one's own creation and review it with dispassion and objectivity was central to Alex's success as an engineer. For example, the serrated front suspension nylon steering bearings, eventually prone to wear, were replaced with external, hinged linkage, as seen on 1950s prototypes but rejected for the more aesthetically pleasing internal linkage. The rear forks now pivoted under the seat tube base, the end of the main frame tube suspended over a simplified "double doughnut" rubber suspension. With some being separable, the Bridgestone offered everything to the 21st century that the first F-frames gave to the 1960's – with the removal of any "achilles heels", liable to be weakened by faulty production, bad servicing or rider abuse. The bikes were made in Japan to a high standard but by the time they were marketed here, the price was too high for them to compete with the small-wheel, utility market, originally created by the Moulton but flooded now with inferior copies. Now the ubiquitous Brompton became the norm on British city streets and a great opportunity was lost. The Brompton fills an important niche in the cycling market and all credit to its inventor, Andrew Ritchie, but, in Alex's words, "Bromptons are for folding, Moultons are for riding"! Perhaps a suitable reply might still be "Maybe its time for the Moulton to excel in *both* fields!"

Looking retrospectively at this book, chapter by chapter, various aspects of the Moulton Bicycle's development can be examined more objectively. For example, built into initial thinking were aerodynamic considerations – cowling and spoke enclosure – and on page 18 we see pre-prototype models with screens, which evolved into the clear, Lexan, Zzipper fairing, launched in 1985, and the fully-faired "pods" such as Doug Milliken's record-breaking "liners", like the 51.29mph record breaking AM. These great achievements fulfilled the early speed attempts made in the 1960s by John Woodburn and others, as described in Chapter 5.

When the Moulton arrived, suspension was virtually unique on a bicycle. It is now commonplace, though normally fitted, either into front forks or hideously large rear springs. It is fitted almost as a fashion accessory rather than born out of a well-considered need to overcome unwanted vibrations from the rigid ride of small wheels. When the RSW arrived to challenge Moulton's success, Raleigh could only overcome this problem with balloon tyres, thus producing a ride which one reviewer described as "like waltzing in gum boots"! To this day, it is true to say that, whereas other cycle manufacturers have fitted rudimentary suspensions, Moulton suspension remains superior.

On p43, we read that some Kirkby-built rear forks suffered overheating in the CO2 welding process. In fact, the problem was more serious still. Many forks were completely lacking in weld or braze at crucial joins and others had severely undercut inner fork blade tubing. Many front suspensions left Kirkby having never been greased – problems that led to drastic failures, further damaging the marque's reputation. These faults are still being discovered and remedied at Moulton Preservation in 2014. None of our restored forks have been returned to us since re-brazing began in 1980, so we can be confident in stating that the faults lay in poor manufacture rather than faulty design. We consider the Series 2 fork an unfortunate substitute. Its very toughness adds weight, subtly alters the F frame angles, eventually causes ovalled pivot holes and, occasionally, even twists or tears the rear of the main frame tube, if rust has weakened that area.

On p49 the "edge-brazed frames" are discussed. We have since learnt that quite a few of these were produced during 1965/6 and often appeared on Moulton Automatics, Continentals and at least one Stowaway. The frames are heavier than their contemporaries and frame numbers usually start 6C or with a curious set of [[= symbols. We know them as the "time warp batch" as they appeared at least 3 years ahead of Raleigh production, which adopted edge brazing on their well-produced "Moulton Major" frames (1968/9). We are still unsure as to whether they were early experiments or intended for export.

Chapter 4 ends considering the "Legacy of the Moulton". The various small-wheelers, made cheaply "in the manner of" the Moulton did the originator no favours, with their inferior ride quality. However, over 30 years later, the proliferation of small-wheelers proves the Moulton concept to be correct and widely adopted for city use. Sadly, the sporting fraternity are still wedded to the provably less-efficient large wheelers, probably due to conservative, macho thinking alone. So, perhaps the true legacy of the Moulton is the Moulton! Continued improvement was always a part of Alex's mission. Today's Moultons are unarguably the most energy efficient form of cycling and possibly even, form of transport! What is needed to fulfil that legacy is the production of an affordable, stowable Moulton; a bike that will hide in a bag or compete in the Race Across America, when, in 1988, Dave Bogdan was the only competitor able to sign his own autograph at the finish, thanks to the smooth AM front suspension!

As Chapter 4 ends, mention is made of Moulton Preservation. Happily, we now offer a wider range of spares than in 1980. Page 150 questions the availability of such items as cable guides and rear suspension pivot assemblies, which are now provided – and we only 'cannibalise' absolute write-offs for spares! So, with improved spares availability, it is all the more tragic that, with the rise of the Internet and eBay, there are opportunistic dealers buying up perfectly good early Moultons, stripping them and selling their components for vast profits. It is less cruel but equally as immoral as killing an elephant to profit from its tusks.

In Chapter 6, the Safari's exceptional carrying capacity is explored. Small wheels and low centre of gravity giving superior – and safer on-board storage. With the coming of the Spaceframe, the ability to pack *within* the frame using protective frame skins, allowed delicate items to be stowed, enclosed in waterproof compartments. Alex prided himself in keeping his pipe and tobacco in the small, front triangle!

Chapter 7 examines the idea of a separable but fully efficient bicycle – The Moulton Stowaway. The Sachs Duomatic hub, that played an essential role in cable-less gearing, re-appeared with the launch of the AM2 "Town" in 1983. But the story goes that, before the Stowaway was launched, Moulton's Company Secretary, John Benjamin ordered a quantity of Sachs hubs and a batch of spares. The hubs arrived, with a terse, Germanic note "Dear Sir, it read, "You will need no spares". This proved absolutely true! Sadly, the same could not be said of the Stowaway joint. An elegant solution in itself, if correctly maintained, but if ridden with the joint loose, permanent damage could occur. A slack joint could give rise to an "arching" sensation upon braking. The AM solution is more robust and foolproof, with several processes to ensure positive locking. It is a clean system on the AM2 but on other AM's, there are cable splitters to consider. The Bridgestone returns to the Stowaway's expander joint system but with a safer, simple rigidity.

For the 21st Century, the issue of stowage versus comfort and performance needs revisiting. Re-evaluating the never-produced M9 Mini Stowaway or adopting Steve Parry's folding rear triangle, pivoting behind a conventional F frame are routes worth exploring. There is work still to be done in order to achieve the perfect, stowable Moulton and this should become central to the marque's future success.

In the Variations chapter, we meet the Mk3. By now, Raleigh owned the Moulton marque, retaining Alex as designer and the Mk3 was the first new offering from this arrangement. In retrospect, the Mk3 can be broadly viewed as a successful link between the F-frame and Spaceframe concept. In particular, the trouble-free, stiffer rear triangle suspension was a leap forward towards what we still see on current Spaceframe Moultons. Had the Mk3 been built with fine componentry rather than accountant-led, cheap gas pipes, it would have been a winner – as exemplified by those restorers who strip off the poor componentry and rebuild according to their taste. The worst component fault on the Mk3 was the S3B hub brake. The seals were always faulty – no amount of tampering seems to stop oil ingressing to the brake shoes, resulting in inefficient braking. The only solution is to disconnect the hub brake and fit a standard calliper to the hole provided on the rear triangle plate.

Although the rear triangle gives a stiffer suspension, we reiterate that, properly fabricated, the original trailing rear fork concept of the Series 1 Moulton remains efficient and provides a delightfully unique ride quality.

At the same time as being asked to contribute to this latest edition of the "Blue Book", I received another request, this time, from Dorling Kindersley Publishers, to provide a good example of the first production Moulton Deluxe. A new book was to be produced, titled *Great Designs*. It includes such things as the Anglepoise lamp, the Aga cooker, the Mini, Citroen DS and Fender Stratocaster guitar. The Moulton Bicycle – in fact, our own, first-preserved, "Miranda", features over *four pages*.

Central to the main page, is a quote from architect, Norman Foster:

"The greatest work of 20th-century British design."

Perhaps, in conclusion, we can celebrate the Moulton as an accepted and revered design icon, so advanced in concept and perfect in function, that, like a natural form – flower or shell, it is inherently beautiful and timeless.

To have helped assure its future has been an honour and I bear witness to the fact that Tony Hadland's book has been instrumental in securing the Moulton's iconic status.

Michael Woolf
co-founder of Moulton Preservation
Chelsea, London
February 2014

INTRODUCTION

The purpose of this book is twofold. On the one hand it aims to introduce the Moulton Bicycle to the many people, cyclists and non-cyclists alike, who either know nothing of it or whose knowledge is limited by the virtual disappearance of this extraordinary machine from our roads; by the numerous myths circulating about it and by the cursory mention it receives in most cycling books. On the other hand it is also hoped that this book will help Moulton owners and devotees to appreciate further the background history and capability of the bike.

My own involvement with the Moulton began when I saw the wife of a local cycle shop proprietor riding her 'Deluxe'. Later, impressed by John Woodburn's record breaking Cardiff – London ride, I purchased a Moulton 'Speed' with which I delivered newspapers. The funds thus raised enabled me to take the bike abroad touring Belgium, Holland, Germany and France.

The 'Speed' was eventually stolen whilst I was a student and lack of funds prevented me replacing it at the time. I drifted away from cycling and when I returned in later years the Moulton had gone out of production. Riding an unsprung 20" wheel machine only increased my hankering after the 'real thing' and, after months of scouring the local classified advertisements, I found a 'Standard' in first class condition which I purchased for £30. Thus, after a break of 8 years I was reunited with the Moulton.

A short time later I read an article about the Moulton in the 'Sunday Times' (30th March 1980). It appeared that I was not the only person still interested in the bike and subsequently I contacted Michael Woolf of Moulton Preservation to suggest that they produce a booklet about the machine. Michael bounced the idea back to me and you are reading the result.

I would like to thank the many people and bodies who have assisted in the production of this book by allowing themselves to be interviewed, by granting me research facilities or by giving permission to reproduce material. They include 'Cycling' magazine, Daved Sanders of the Moulton Bicycle

Club, Michael Woolf of Moulton Preservation, the Design Council, Raleigh Industries and John Woodburn. Special thanks must also go to Alex Moulton Limited for the research facilities afforded to me and for their permission to reproduce illustrations. Company Secretary, John Benjamin dealt with my many queries most patiently, but in no way attempted to impair the objectivity of the text.

Finally I must express my deep gratitude to Mike Radford and John Pinkerton, both of the Southern Veteran–Cycle Club. Without their assistance this edition would not have been possible.

Tony Hadland

Additional Reading

Mark Ottaway. 'Scene – Yesterday's Bike of the Future' The Sunday Times 30th March 1980, p. 50. This article was a major catalyst in the present revival of interest in the Moulton (Illustrated).

CHAPTER 1

THE INVENTOR (AND THE RUBBER CONNECTION)

The Moulton Bicycle was very much the product of one man's creative thinking and hence it is relevant to examine the background of that man, Dr. Alex Moulton.

Originally the Moultons were of Devon sea-faring stock, but by the 18th century a branch of the family had moved to London where Alex Moulton's great-great-great-grandfather was a broker. His son was a printer who in turn raised a son by the name of Stephen. In middle-age Stephen emigrated to the United States where he became a broker in New York. He became a friend of Charles Goodyear who discovered the rubber vulcanisation process. Stephen returned to England and tried to sell the Goodyear process but to no avail and so, at the age of 52, he decided to go into rubber production himself.

In 1848 he bought 'The Hall' at Bradford-on-Avon together with its derelict cloth mill which he converted to rubber production. The house, built about 1610, has been described as 'among the finest of the smaller houses of its age' by 'Country Life' and in 1900 was the model for the British Pavilion at the Paris Exhibition.

The Hall, Bradford-on-Avon

Stephen Moulton, having established his rubber mill, never looked back and one of the earliest uses of his rubber technology was in the waterproof capes used by British soldiers in the Crimean War. In fact his technical expertise was highly regarded by contemporary engineers such as Brunel and Stephenson. He died in 1880, aged 86, with the family seat and fortune soundly established.

Forty years later his great-grandson Alex was born. The boy was educated at Marlborough and later at King's College, Cambridge where he graduated in engineering. During the Second World War he was employed in the Engine Research Department of the Bristol Aeroplane Company where for two years he was personal assistant to Sir Roy Fedden, the Chief Engineer.

After the War he returned to the family rubber firm, George Spencer, Moulton and Co. Ltd., where he established a research department specialising in rubber suspension systems for vehicles. During this time he invented a type of trailer suspension, the 'Flexitor', which is still produced at Bradford-on-Avon.

In 1956 the family business was sold to the Avon Rubber Company and Alex Moulton founded Moulton Developments Limited in order to concentrate on creative design and development of suspension systems. The old stable block at 'The Hall' was converted into engineering workshops, a modern drawing office was erected nearby and the administration office was established in part of the mansion itself.

Sculptured in Portland Stone by Barry Baldwin in 1974. The Plaque measures 24" x 30" and is situated on the Bicycle Factory. It depicts Tom Simpson testing the Moulton Bicycle in 1963.

The British Motor Corporation took a financial interest in the new company and for two decades enjoyed exclusive manufacturing rights for Moulton automobile suspension systems. This partnership resulted in the evolution of the rubber suspension used in the Mini and the fluid interconnected 'Hydrolastic' system, first used on the Austin/Morris 1100/1300 range in 1962. Later the 'Hydragas' system, found in the Austin Allegro and Princess, was developed from the 'Hydrolastic' suspension by replacing its rubber springs with gas sprung units. Indeed a modified version of 'Hydragas' springing is used in the new Austin Metro, and the much acclaimed 1982 Austin Ambassador also rides on Moulton suspension.

The Moulton Company now act as worldwide consultants in the field of automobile suspension technology. British Leyland, the descendant of BMC, no longer has a financial holding in the Company.

Dr. Moulton's work in the field of suspension design has been accomplished simultaneously with his development of the Moulton bicycle which began in 1958. He holds the opinion that one is capable of pursuing two main avenues of research simultaneously but no more.

Alex Moulton's leisure pursuits include cycling, canoeing and shooting. He is also fascinated by steam power and operates his own steam launch. Entitled to use at least nine sets of letters after his name, he is a Commander of the British Empire, a Royal Designer to Industry, an Honorary Doctor of the Royal College of Arts, an Honorary Doctor of Science at Bath University and has been admitted to the Fellowship of Engineering. He has also published numerous articles and papers on engineering and education.

Additional Reading – Primary Sources

A). 'Alex Moulton and his Mini Wheeled "Full Sized" Bicycles' Car Styling Quarterly, April 1974 (Japan). A first-class, well illustrated article (in Japanese with English translation) on the evolution of the Moulton bicycle. The first part of the text, entitled 'Gentleman of Wiltshire' covers the Moulton family background in detail.

B). 'Moulton Rubber' The Motor, 4th September 1963 pp 52–55. An excellent detailed biography of Alex Moulton (Illustrated).

C). Patrick MacNaughten. 'Moulton Rubber' Motor Trade Executive, c. 1963. A brief description of the background and philosophy of the Moulton organisation. (Illustrated).

D). Arthur Oswald. 'The Hall, Bradford-on-Avon' Country Life, 11th October 1962, pp 840–843 and 18th October 1962 pp 900 – 904. A good description of the Moulton residence and its surroundings (Illustrated).

E). 'Country Homes and Gardens, Old and New – The Hall, Bradford-on-Avon' Country Life Illustrated, 11th March 1899 pp 304–308. As D). above but when the seat of Mr. John Moulton. (Illustrated).

F). 'Biographical Precis' Alex Moulton Limited, March 1979.

G). 'Notes on Dr. Moulton and Moulton Developments Limited' Alex Moulton Limited (Undated untitled draft).

H). Entry in "Who's Who 1980' under Moulton, Alexander Eric CBE 1976, RDI.

CHAPTER 2

INCEPTION

When the Moulton Bicycle was launched late in 1962 it represented one of the few serious attempts to improve on the established diamond frame design.

The familiar 'Big Wheeler' owes its origins largely to J.K. Starley[1] whose 1888 'Rover' bicycle featured a diamond frame albeit composed of curved tubes and lacking a seat tube. By 1890 the Humber 'Safety' had a frame which was similar in most respects to that found on the majority of present day machines. It is a testimony to the inherent soundness of the diamond frame that for some 90 years it has dominated cycling world-wide.

From time to time various new bicycle designs have been launched such as the renowned hammock-saddled 'Dursley-Pedersen' and the Belgian shaft drive 'Fabrique Nationale'. Before the Moulton perhaps the most serious attack on the conventional bicycle design came from the recumbent machines of the 1930's, particularly the 'Velocar' which broke most contemporary short-distance track records[2]. However, these machines faded into oblivion and for the most part are relegated to museums and veteran cycle rallies. It was up to Alex Moulton to mount the next serious challenge.

It appears that Moulton first made public the thinking behind his design in an address to the Pedal Club on 14th November 1962, shortly after the new bicycle was launched at the Cycle and Motor Cycle Show.

Alex Moulton had enjoyed cycle touring whilst at school, continued cycling whilst at University and had eventually progressed to ownership of a first-class lightweight machine made by Hetchins. He became curious as to how the bicycle could be further developed and so in 1957 began investigating the best riding position.

This study included obtaining one of the old recumbent machines of the 1930's, (a Grubb). Although this offered minimum wind resistance, the very low position was considered unacceptable as it led to considerable thigh fatigue when ridden for long periods. The completely upright stance was also rejected, the final decision being in favour of the conventional racing position. By this means the relationship between the pedals, saddle and handlebars was established.

The drive system was also investigated. In the last century at least two machines, the 'Facile' and the Singer 'Xtraordinary' employed lever drive systems and in 1883 J.H. Adams broke the 24 hour speed record on a 'Facile'. Alex Moulton investigated swinging lever systems and was apparently still interested in their possibilities when the Moulton Bicycle was launched. Although no Moulton was ever marketed with lever drive transmission, it is interesting to note that an American machine is now available thus equipped.

One of the many areas investigated by Alex Moulton was wheel size. Many early bicycles had very large wheels, the front wheel of the 'Ordinary' or 'Penny Farthing' usually being around 52" in diameter. The conventional modern bicycle generally has 26" or 27" wheels. Moulton observed that in all other forms of wheeled transport, such as railway locomotives and motor vehicles, there had been a continuous, gradual reduction in wheel size since the turn of the century.

With the assistance of the Dunlop Rubber Company, with whom Moulton Consultants had close business links, tests were conducted on 14" and 16" x 1 3/8" wheels. It was found that, if reasonably high tyre pressures of around 60 p.s.i. were adopted, such bicycle wheels would roll just as easily as the larger diameter conventional type of similar cross section running at the pressures typically used by utility cyclists[3].

Experiments with Wheels
Left; wheel with spokes enclosed to reduce turbulence.
Centre; foreground; wheel fairing
Centre; background; solid tyred wheel
Right: glass-fibre spoked wheel
(Photo by Author).

The smaller wheels were found to possess many inherent advantages including tremendous mechanical strength, enhanced acceleration due to the light mass of the wheel (and hence lower inertia), and the ability to construct a machine with a much lower centre of gravity particularly when carrying a considerable quantity of luggage.

The great problem posed by the adoption of a small wheel size was the very bumpy ride which would inevitably ensue. A small wheel tends to fall and rise more rapidly when it encounters depressions and bumps in a road surface. It also tends to fall deeper into some holes than would a larger wheel. With a rigid frame this would lead to a greater loss of forward momentum as well. A large wheeled conventional bicycle is hardly the most comfortable means of transport and a rigid-framed small wheeler is worse still. One solution to the problem would be to use balloon tyres but these have a poor rolling resistance and would have resulted in a machine slower than the conventional bicycle.

The Mk I Monocoque, 1959 outside The Hall, Bradford-on-Avon.

Some form of springing was required and the first experimental Moulton bicycle, built in 1959, had 14" wheels with a trailing link type fork suspension for the front wheel[4]. The 'frame' of this machine was of monocoque[5] construction using 22 gauge duralumin. This form of construction arose from Moulton's quest for rigidity which he found lacking in conventional lightweight bicycles which can be prone to whip. This can lead to dangerous 'speed wobble' especially when descending hills and is worsened if the machine is carrying panniers.

The Monocoque Moulton was the result of many aerodynamically styled scale models. It was lively and responsive and the body weighed only 5½lbs. but it produced unacceptable road noise. It also required a sub-frame to carry the heavily loaded components of the transmission system and its appearance was not very attractive.

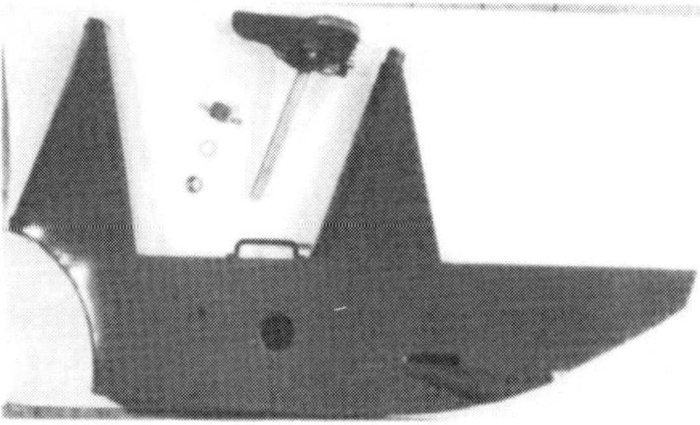

The main 'Frame' of the Mk I Monocoque.

Experiments then followed with many different frame designs including at least two constructed of laminated timber. Some three dozen variations were tried before the final production frame was evolved. Soon after abandoning the Monocoque experiment a 'Lazy F' frame was produced out of 20 gauge 2" diameter mild steel. This was fitted with glass-fibre mouldings at both ends for weather protection. The front suspension was retained but used rubber in compression (as opposed to tension as was the case with the earlier machine). Carriers were fitted to the front and rear and the wheel size was increased to 16". Two main points arose from the experiments with this machine. The round section tubing was prone to whip and the front suspension showed up the lack of any at the rear. Fitting deeper saddle springs to improve rider comfort was rejected as it reduced pedalling efficiency and so the decision was made to fit rear wheel suspension.

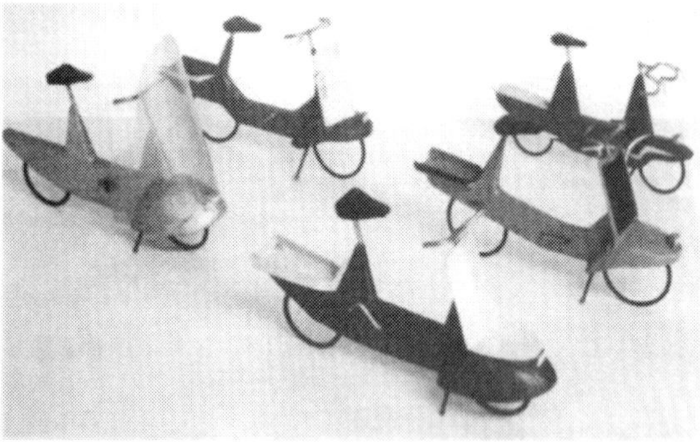

The search for form – pre-prototype models.

Alex Moulton was also experimenting with aerodynamic cowlings at this time. It was found that these made a definite contribution to ease of cycling as well as providing better weather protection but they were abandoned because they were considered too cumbersome for the average rider. Experiments were conducted into the use of solid tyres and the effects of enclosing the spokes with glass-fibre dishes to reduce air turbulence. One of the experimental bicycles incorporated an adjustable steering head to help establish the best frame geometry.

Early prototype Moultons featured a leading arm or Earl's type suspension for the front wheel with the rubber spring unit behind the wheel. This produced unacceptable steering characteristics and it became apparent that a system which concentrated all the mass around the steering axis was required. The twin telescopic system used on most motorbikes would have been too complex, heavy and unsightly.

Leading arm front suspension on a prototype Moulton (Photo by author).

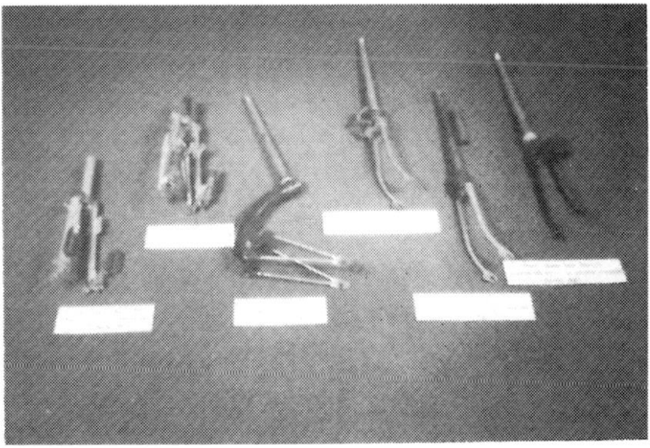

Evolutionary prototype front suspension systems.

Alex Moulton's solution was simple yet effective. After much research and development a system was devised whereby a splined steel column was mounted on the crown of the forks. This column passed through a nylon bush which could withstand approximately half-a-million vibrations without noticeable wear. (Earlier prototypes utilised a triple hinged steel steering link behind the rubber bellows in order to connect the fork crown to the steering column). The steel column was mounted on a column of rubber (contained within the steel column) which extended into the steering tube. The rubber supported 80% of the load, the remainder being carried by a coil spring which was wound round the rubber. The clearances were so adjusted that the rubber was deformed into compression discs by the spring coils thus stabilising the column and providing friction damping.

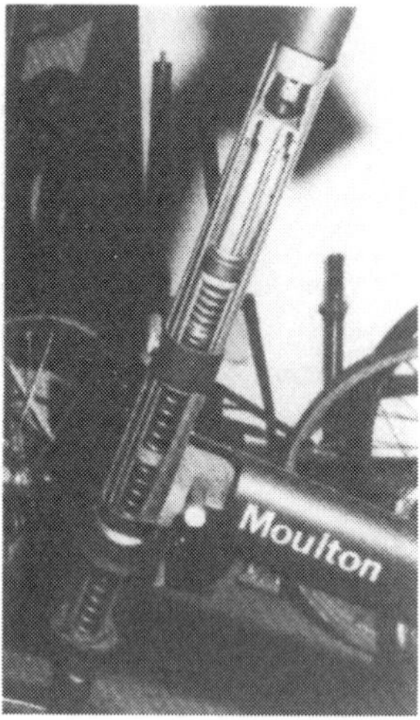

The production suspension systems – shown above and top right – in a cutaway 'Series Two' Moulton. (Photo by author).

The rear suspension was less of a problem and in the final prototype consisted of a swinging arm type with phosphor-bronze bearings. (In later production machines nylon bearings were used). The rubber springing unit was a metal-to-rubber bonded type which fitted into the end of the main frame tube. The rubber sandwich was curved but its radius did not coincide with that of the pivot. Hence the movement was not entirely in shear but as deflection increased more compression component came in with a consequent steepening of the rate curve. Thus a wide range of loads could be catered for ranging from a large child to a 6' 2" adult with 70 lbs of luggage.

The evolution of the Moulton trailing arm rear suspension.

Before the popularisation of the pneumatic tyre a number of sprung frame bicycle designs were evolved. In fact the Matchless 'Highwheeler' c. 1884 had rubber suspension of a sort to both wheel bearings, the handlebar fixing and the saddle mounting. These early attempts at springing obviously aimed at producing a more comfortable ride and some early bicycle engineers seem to have understood that, by minimising the unsprung mass of machine and rider, less effort should be required when riding over rough surfaces. However, practical difficulties were experienced with respect to incorporating good damping and minimising wear of the moving parts. So much so that with the coming of mass produced pneumatic tyres and better road surfaces most work on bicycle suspension systems ceased.

Since the First World War few attempts have been made at producing bicycles with suspension. An otherwise conventional machine with sprung wheels was demonstrated by being ridden down a flight of stairs at a West German trade fair shortly after the Second World War but thereafter seems to have disappeared without trace. In the 1950's some British schoolboys fitted sprung moped front forks to their bicycles for use in 'Bog Wheeling' an early form of bicycle moto-cross. On the other side of the Atlantic Captain Dan Henry of the U.S.A. produced a lightweight big wheeler with coil springing in the late 1960's. This machine was never commercially produced although it was demonstrated to Raleigh. It is claimed to have performed well and Captain Henry also produced a recumbent bicycle with suspension.

With the recent popularity of bicycle moto-cross a few BMX machines have been marketed with suspension but these are specialised juvenile machines unsuitable for serious use on the road. However, back in the late 1950's when Alex Moulton was carrying out his experiments, the idea of a bicycle incorporating independent suspension was almost unheard of[6].

The design of a workable suspension system for a serious bicycle involves considerable technical problems. It must be lightweight and relatively maintenance free. It must be capable of operating satisfactorily under a wide range of loading conditions. No significant play should be introduced into the steering system and no appreciable power loss should be possible. This last point is particularly important as, with a poorly designed system, a considerable amount of the rider's energy could be wasted in simply bouncing the machine on its springs. Moulton's design overcame these problems and it was thus possible to utilise the advantages of the 16" wheel with high pressure tyres whilst offering a ride which was considerably smoother under most conditions than that offered by the conventional bicycle.

Having resolved the problem of the suspension, Alex Moulton turned his attention to the best wheelbase length and concluded that one about 3" longer than usual would produce smoother running without torsion problems especially when braking. Hence a wheelbase of 44½" was selected.

Evolution of the 'Lazy F' frame continued and this was so designed that the saddle could be raised or lowered without the use of a spanner to cover the traditional frame sizes from 19¾" to 25". Furthermore the Moulton had no cross-bar in the traditional sense and hence started the modern trend for multi-adjustable unisex bicycles. Neither the open frame[7] nor the unisex feature was without precedent. Dan Albone produced a large wheeled cross-frame machine called the 'Ivel' in 1886 and several other manufacturers, including Humber, produced similar designs about that time. Humber and Quadrant both produced a tricycle in the 1890's which was convertible for use by both sexes and as late as 1930 James produced a bicycle and a tandem rear section which could be converted for male or female use. However, Alex Moulton's new frame design required no conversion and permitted easier mounting and dismounting than earlier open frame designs whilst being substantially more rigid than a conventional ladies bicycle.

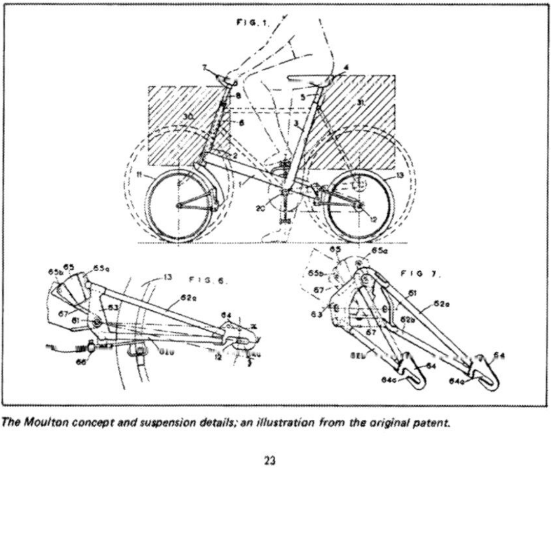

The Moulton concept and suspension details; an illustration from the original patent.

The constructional methods finally adopted to assemble the Moulton were unorthodox being more reminiscent of aircraft construction than of traditional bicycle frame building. Alex Moulton's earlier experience with the Bristol Aeroplane Company was no doubt an influence here. Tapered and flat sided tubes were used and Moulton's collaborated with Tube Products of Oldbury in creating manipulating techniques to allow lugless and riveted construction. (The rivets were not used primarily for mechanical strength but in order to correctly position the frame components during the brazing process). Mild steel ERW tube was finally adopted for the production models.

The integral carrier system of the final design was another notable feature. The carrying of loads on the conventional bicycle has always been a problem. Panniers are of somewhat restricted capacity and can introduce considerable whip into the handling of a bicycle, especially downhill. Handlebar bags and conventional front carriers can adversely affect the steering. Saddlebags are of restricted capacity and mounted high on the machine. The construction and fixing of many carrier systems is also rather poor. Large loads can be carried on conventional machines but the rider always suffers from the disadvantage that the bicycle was designed first and the bags and carriers are merely an afterthought. The Moulton, on the other hand, was specifically designed to carry loads with securely integrated carriers. The front carrier is fixed to the frame and hence does not affect the steering. It can carry 20 lbs. of luggage whereas the rear carrier can master 50 lbs. There is no trace of whip and, if anything, the road-holding is better with a load on than without.

The final design having been established prototypes were constructed and extensively tested, even on wet ice. At last the Moulton bicycle was ready to be offered to the public but first a manufacturer had to be found. Alex Moulton always wanted Raleigh to make the machine and many of their executives were keen to take it on. Indeed some of Moulton's development work was done at Nottingham in conjunction with Raleigh.However, the sales department thought that there would be little market for an overgrown 'Fairy Cycle' without a cross-bar and their influence was to prove decisive. Raleigh turned the Moulton down.

Subsequently Alex Moulton commissioned a Market Research Survey 'As far away from the bicycle industry . . . as possible' – in Irvine, near Glasgow. Contrary to the expectations of the cycle trade, the public reaction to the Moulton bicycle was overwhelmingly positive.

Alex Moulton then decided that if the world's largest bicycle maker would not produce his machine then he would. A production unit was established at Bradford-on-Avon and within a comparatively short time Moulton Bicycles Limited became the second largest frame manufacturers in Britain.

John Emery testing a prototype Moulton at Southampton in January 1962.

The original Moulton bicycle factory in the grounds of The Hall, Bradford-on-Avon, 1963.

Notes

1). Many books and articles credit James Starley's 1885 'Safety' as being the precursor of the modern diamond frame design. However, he died in 1881 and his nephew, variously referred to as John or James Kemp Starley, produced the 1885 'Rover' which had indirect steering and only vaguely resembled the modern bicycle. The direct steering version was introduced in 1888.

2). Recumbent machines seem to be making a minor comeback particularly in short-distance speed trials. Three contemporary U.S. machines are the Vector, Willkie and Avatar. The latter is manufactured by Fomac Inc., 40 Oakdale Road, Wilmington, Massachusetts 01887, U.S.A.

3). An interesting open frame bicycle of strangely modern appearance was photographed on the streets of occupied Paris by the Nazi photo-magazine 'Signal!'. The wheels appear to have been about 16" in diameter with narrow section tyres and the caption stated that 'This practical construction is easier to propel than an ordinary machine but one needs a certain amount of nonchalance in order to appear with it on the street'.

4). A 'link' in this context is a sprung near-horizontal arm with a pivot at one end and a wheel axle at the other. A 'leading link' is one where the pivot is behind the wheel axle relative to the usual direction of travel. Conversely a 'trailing link' is one with the wheel axle behind the pivot e.g. the rear suspension of most Moulton bicycles.

5). The term 'monocoque' generally means that the body of a vehicle is used to withstand all or most of the forces to which it is subject without recourse to a separate load-bearing frame or chassis. e.g. most lorries have a chassis but almost all private cars are now of monocoque construction.

6). In 1982 the 'Brompton' folding bicycle was launched. This incorporates a rear suspension system very similar to that used on the Moulton 'MK III'. Details are available from Brompton Bicycle (Sales) Ltd., The Old Powerhouse, Kew Gardens Station, Richmond, Surrey.

7). An 'open frame' means one without a cross-bar in the usual sense. One such design was the cross-frame which, in crude terms, had a main beam linking the steering head to the rear wheel and another member, approximately at right angles, linking saddle and bottom bracket.

Additional Reading – Primary Sources

A). 'The Bicycle Revived by Fresh Design' Engineering, 9th November 1962. A particularly good article on the evolution of the Moulton bicycle. (Illustrated).

B). 'How a Design was Born' Cycling, 23rd May 1964. Describes the evolution of the Moulton up to the stage when the company was the second largest frame builder under one name in Britain. (Illustrated).

C). P.W. Allen, P.B. Lindley, A.R. Payne (Editors) 'Use of Rubber in Engineering'. Maclaren 1967. This conference abstract contains an interesting chapter by Dr. A.E. Moulton entitled 'The Moulton Suspension Systems' covering the automotive and bicycle systems. (Illustrated).

D). 'How I Planned the New Bicycle' Cycling, 21st November 1962. A report of Alex Moulton's address to the Pedal Club on 14th November 1962.

E). Richard Carr. 'Design Analysis' Design No. 176, 1963 pp 42–45. A comprehensive report on the Moulton, the first part of which covers the design philosophy and evolutionary aspects. (Illustrated).

F). See Chapter 1 Additional Reading, A). Page 130 covers the development of the Moulton Bicycle. (Illustrated).

– Secondary Sources

G). F.R. Whitt, D.G. Wilson. 'Bicycling Science' MIT Press 1974 pp 124–131. This section describes the use of antivibration devices in bicycles from the pre-pneumatic tyre era to the present day (Illustrated).

H). R. John Way. 'The Bicycle' Hamlyn 1973. Contains an interesting, well illustrated chapter on bicycle history but repeats the error mentioned in Note 1). above.

I). Derek Roberts. 'This Veteran Business' Southern Veteran–Cycle Club. 3rd Edition May 1979. An excellent booklet giving a concise history of bicycle evolution. (Illustrated).

J). Allan Hawkes. 'Bicycle History and the Moulton' Moulton Cyclist No. 14, January 1981. This article relates the Moulton to earlier bicycle designs.

K). 'La Premier Bicyclette Nouvelle Depuis 70 Ans' Le Cycle, August/September 1965 (France). A two part feature in French on the history of the Moulton bicycle up to 1965.

L). As G). above pp 71 and 96. Refers to and illustrates the 'Velocar' recumbent bicycle.

M). As G). above pp 71–75. Comments on the relative efficiency of reclining pedalling machines.

N). S.L. Mayer (Editor). 'Signal! – Hitler's Wartime Picture Magazine' Bison Books 1976. A feature entitled 'Paris on Wheels' includes the photograph referred to in Note 3). above.

– **Video**

O). 'Materials and Mechanics – The Moulton Bicycle' Open University, recorded 2nd February 1972. 1st transmission 12th March 1972, repeated 16th March 1972. Tape No. VTM/6LT/70383.
This 20 minute monochrome videotape was produced by Tony Jolly as part of a course unit entitled 'Structures and Microstructures'. It was recorded in the museum at The Hall and features Dr. Moulton explaining the development of his ideas. The tape is not available for general hire.

CHAPTER 3

LAUNCH AND SUCCESS

'Impact' was the heading of the Editorial of 'Cycling' Magazine when it reported on the launch of the Moulton bicycle in November 1962 at the Earls Court Cycle and Motor Cycle Show.

The Editorial contrasted the Moulton with other innovative bicycle designs of the past and concluded that the new bike stood up well to scrutiny and was reasonably priced. The Editor also decided that the lines of the Moulton were 'not too far removed from that other fashion setter of recent years, the Scooter'.

The Moulton certainly dominated the 1962 Cycle Show. 'Cycling' published a photograph of Alex Moulton explaining the workings of the machine to Lord Brabazon of Tara and the Show President, Edward Turner. David Duffield[1] of Moulton Bicycles was reported as stating that the reaction was 'fantastic' and orders had been placed by Lady Rothschild, Lord Cadenham, Lord Montagu and Lord Hailsham (Quintin Hogg, the Conservative Cabinet Minister who became a regular Moulton cyclist to the delight of the tabloid press). Enquiries were received from all over the world including Antigua.

In fact, public reaction to the new bicycle was so strong that Alex Moulton telephoned Bradford-on-Avon from the Cycle Show to order the doubling in size of his factory. Sir Leonard Lord (later Lord Lambury), the Head of the British Motor Corporation, offered his production facilities to Moulton. This well-intentioned offer eventually led to the concentration of Moulton manufacture at Kirkby where quality control was so poor. It is ironic to reflect that, at the very launch of the new bicycle, one of the seeds was sown of its eventual disappearance.

The models shown at the Cycle Show included the 'Standard', 'Deluxe', 'Speed', 'Stowaway' and 'Safari' The price tags varied from £25. 9s. 6d. for the collapsible 'car boot' 'Stowaway' to £43. 19s. 6d. for the fully equipped tourist version, the 'Safari'.

The 1962 Cycle Show; Alex Moulton (extreme right) explains his revolutionary bicycle to Lord Brabazon of Tara, Show President Edward Turner, and left, H.B. Yates. The bicycle is on a 'Bump Rig' to demonstrate the suspension. (Photo courtesy of 'Cycling').

'Cycling' Magazine carried some excellent 'in depth' articles on the Moulton. One, entitled 'Bold Attack on the Diamond Frame' (7th November, 1962) commented on the reactions of a cross-section of riders from amongst the general public all of which were favourable (this tallied with Moulton's own market research carried out in the streets of Western Scotland). The writer commented on the 'girder like quality' of the main tube on which the 'Lazy F' frame was based. He described the greater safety resulting from the lower centre of gravity and the integral carriers. The greater rigidity and strength of the 16" wheels was noted and the suspension system was hailed as contributing significantly to both the safety factor and the comfort of the rider. To quote from the article, 'the design is such that no sponginess is experienced, nor does the front suspension permit twist or whip in the steering. A certain amount of "lift" is present when pulling hard on the handlebars to ascend steep hills; this is disconcerting at first but neither safety nor efficiency is impaired and one soon gets used to applying a revised style of approach to gradients.'

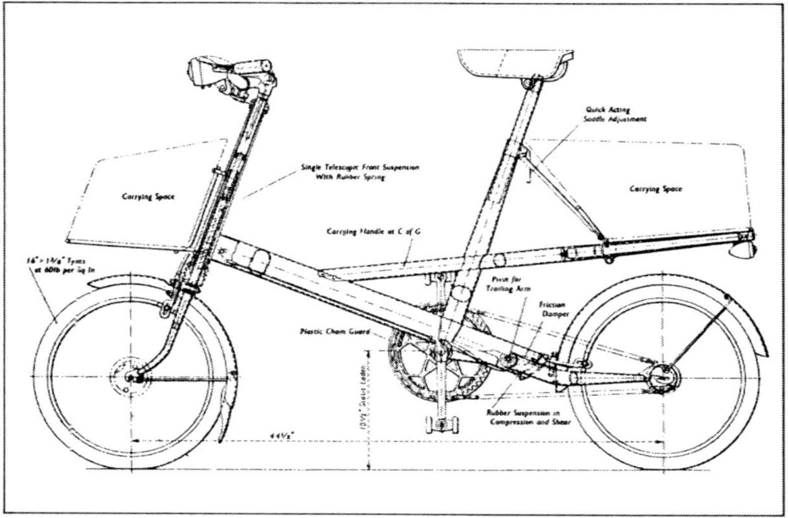

General arrangement engineering drawing of 'Series One' Moulton bicycle.

The riveted and brazed frame construction was described and accompanying photographs showed details of the frame construction and also a completely dismantled front suspension unit. The writer also noted that a greater feeling of security resulted from the braking on the Moulton. This was put down to the brake position being closer to the ground than on the conventional machine. (My own feeling is that it is related largely to the longer wheelbase, the lower mass of the wheels and the tendency of the front suspension to absorb part of the machine's momentum when braking).

The article made the point that, although lightweight racing versions had been manufactured, the main aim of the Moulton company was to create a new market for utility machines. The writer concluded by stating that 'of all the sensational designs for a generation it seems to have the most to commend it'.

Accompanying the article was a detailed specification of the prototype 'Deluxe' which at the time of its launch was scheduled to sell at £31 19s. 6d. It weighed 34½ lb. and incorporated several features which were altered in the production model. For instance, the front fork rake was 2¼" rather than the 1" of production 'Deluxes' and the rear carrier incorporated a reflector and side guards to retain the holdall, features which were not found in any production Moulton. This bicycle also had a three speed hub gear as opposed to the four speed fitted to the production model and no front carrier was provided.

Another article on the Moulton appeared in 'Cycling's' 'Lightweight Man' feature. This showed a cutaway drawing of the front suspension unit and the writer commented on Alex Moulton's achievements in automotive suspension design. The 'Lightweight Man' wrote of riding prototypes of the Moulton Bicycle 'over a pothole-pocked road that would have found me carrying my normal 27" wheeled bicycle'. He also enthused over the Moulton's luggage carrying capacity and its manoeuvrability, stating that it permitted a 'U' turn in half the usual radius'. He concluded by stating that the Moulton was 'no gimmick but has been well thought out by a cyclist of experience, a scientist unbounded by the narrow confines of convention'.

'Cycling' magazine's coverage also included perspective sketches of the 'Break Joint' mechanism in the main beam of the Moulton 'Stowaway', the quick release seat pin toggle and the rear suspension unit. An interesting point here is that the sketch shows a rear suspension friction damper, adjusted by means of 'C' spanners. In practice the only production model marketed with this feature was the 'Safari' tourer although the later 'Speedsix' incorporated similar dampers adjusted by flat-jawed spanners.

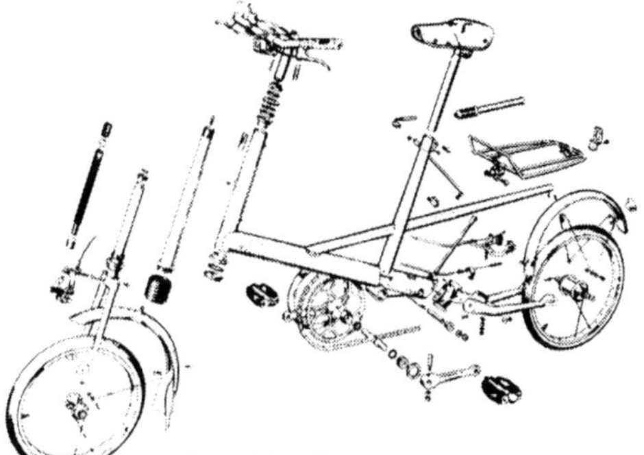

Explcded view of Moulton bicycle.

Moulton "Stowaway" cycle.

Moulton cycle seat pin toggle.

Moulton De Luxe cycle.

Detail sketches of the Moulton as printed in 'Cycling' magazine, December 1962.

'Design' magazine (No. 176, 1963) also gave very good coverage to the new bicycle in the form of a six page design analysis by Richard Carr. This recorded the evolution of the Moulton and the design philosophy behind it. The claimed advantages of better road holding, superior acceleration, enhanced manoeuvrability, greater comfort and improved luggage carrying capacity were subjectively tested and most of the claims substantiated. But 'Design' went further and had the suspension system scientifically tested by EMI Electronics Ltd. The testers concluded that at very low speed the Moulton transmitted slightly more all-round vibration than a conventional machine but that in general the peak road shock levels were halved by the Moulton suspension system. It was also noted that the efficiency of the suspension improved the faster the bike was ridden and the heavier it was loaded. 'Design' had slight reservations about the light steering, which took some getting used to at low speeds, but on the whole gave the Moulton high praise. The point was made 'that its designer has taken the trouble to rethink bicycle design afresh and develop a machine which makes a complete break with established concepts'.

So it was, that with considerable free publicity, the Moulton bicycle was launched. Production began at Bradford-on-Avon in March 1963 and success was quick to follow. The Moulton became fashionable, a mini-bike to go with mini-skirts and mini-cars, all part of the "Swinging 60's".

In an article entitled 'Spending Money on Things to Change your Life in 1963' "Queen" Magazine praised the Moulton for its 'marvellous long low shape'. The architectural critic Reyner Banham enthused over the Moulton in the pages of the 'New Statesman' in November 1963 and the 'Sunday Times' 'Fashion on the Move' feature showed four photographs of the Hon. Mrs. de Laszlo visiting the coiffeur on her Moulton 'Deluxe' (16th Feburary 1964). The 'Evening Standard' for 10th November 1965 printed a cartoon by JAK in which a smugly aloof Moulton cyclist is seen cruising past fuming motorists held up in traffic. The caption reads 'Is this Lord Rothschild, Mr. Marples, Lonnie Donegan, Terry Downs? No it's me on their sort of bike!'.

The October/November 1965 edition of 'Road Safety' tested the Moulton and concluded that it 'is mighty and represents the most practical advance in safety for cyclists in recent years'.

The Bradford-on-Avon factory showing use of special reversible brazing jigs (1965–6). (Photo courtesy of I.P.C. Business Press).

The sporting successes, described in the chapter 'Moulton Speed', helped boost the new bicycle reputation and Lord Montagu acquired a replica of the Moulton which broke the Cardiff-London record for display in his Transport Museum at Beaulieu. London's Science Museum soon featured a Moulton 'Safari' as the latest stage in the evolution of the bicycle. (This has now been replaced by a Moulton MKIII). The Design Centre gave the Moulton an award and the bicycle also won a Gold Medal at the International Milan Triennale, the F.H. Bidlake Memorial Trophy and the Ambassador Award for achievement in industry. Moulton Developments were later given the Queen's award to Industry for their work on automotive suspension systems and the new bicycle.

Sales of the Moulton Bicycle were good and production eventually exceeded 1,000 units a week. A total of over 100,000 had been made by the time the British Motor Corporation took full control of production in 1966. By that time the Moulton was being exported on a modest scale to 30 countries and built under licence in the United States, Australia and Norway. Even Raleigh were producing Moultons under licence in South Africa, these being equipped with 1 5/8" tyres for use on dirt roads.

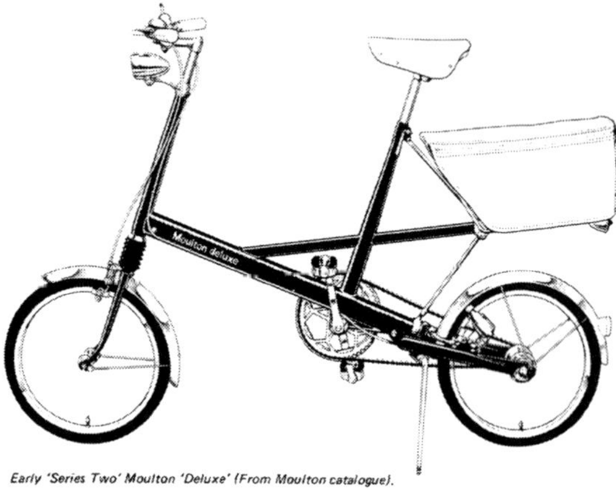

Early 'Series Two' Moulton 'Deluxe' (From Moulton catalogue).

After the launch in late 1962 the range of models offered rapidly expanded to seven plus three high specification 'S' range variants. The chapter 'Variations' describes the various models in detail.

Before the introduction of the Moulton the cycle industry had been in the doldrums. The late fifties and early sixties had seen many families becoming car owners for the first time and fewer people were dependent on the bicycle as a basic means of transport. The Moulton brought something of a bonanza to the retail bicycle trade. At one time whole cycle shop windows were to be seen full of Moultons and the turnover was quick. Apart from sales of conventional lightweight sports cycles, the established bicycle makers were doing badly. Not only were they missing out on the new 'mini-bike' boom but their already depleted market in utility bicycles had been drastically reduced.

They desperately needed to produce a 'Moulton' of their own but the key to the new bicycle's success was its patented suspension system permitting the use of narrow section high pressure tyres. While rival manufacturers scrutinised the small print of Alex Moulton's patents and Raleigh lived with the knowledge that they had let the prize slip through their hands, Moulton Bicycles became the second largest frame makers in the country.

During the mid-sixties Duff Hart-Davis wrote several articles in the 'Sunday Telegraph' about small-wheeled bicycles. He described the merits of travelling around London by Moulton in an article entitled 'Enjoy London by Mini-Bike' published in 1967. Hart-Davis wrote of carrying a 60 lb. crate of oranges across London on his bicycle and he noted the widely differing attitudes of the doormen at Harrods and the Savoy to patrons arriving by Moulton. He also remarked on the comments of cockney wits such as 'Cor - you ain't arf worn them wheels down mate!'.

In July 1965 Duff Hart-Davis had written an article in the 'Sunday Telegraph' entitled 'Mini-bike Madness' describing his road test of Raleigh's long awaited answer to the Moulton, the 'RSW 16'. This bicycle was given an unprecedented £100,000 publicity launch on 17th July 1965 and was announced as 'The new revolutionary RSW16 by Raleigh – the answer to all short haul transport problems. Easy to handle, simple to park and designed for modern living. Instantly adjusted to suit any size of rider'. The initials 'RSW 16' stood for Raleigh Small Wheels 16" and this machine was bad news for the Moulton and, some would argue, for cycling generally.

Raleigh's answer to the Moulton – the RSW 16. This is the original press release photo.

Unable to circumvent Alex Moulton's patents Raleigh had produced a somewhat similar-looking machine which undercut the Moulton on price. The basic model corresponded in many ways with the Moulton 'Deluxe' in specification. It had a universal open frame and spannerless adjustment of not only the saddle but also the handlebars. However, the seat height could not accommodate the larger adults as well as could the Moulton and the handlebars were so designed that no variation of reach or style was possible. A rear carrier with quick-release holdall was provided as standard but no front carrier facility was provided. The bicycle came fitted with Sturmey-Archer 3 speed gears (twist-grip operated) and Dynohub lighting, the headlamp being fitted to the front mudguard and the tail lamp built into the rear mudguard. An integral propstand and conventional chainguard were also fitted but it was the wheels which provided the biggest shock.

Unable to produce a competitive suspension system without contravening Moulton's patents Raleigh had resorted to 2" diameter balloon tyres running at a lower pressure of around 35 p.s.i. They effectively sacrificed the easier running of the high pressure narrow tyres used on the Moulton for a tyre which had much greater rolling resistance but looked comfortable to the uninformed potential purchaser[2].

The absence of a suspension system meant that the 'RSW 16' was cheaper to produce and its full specification, good quality finish and competitive price, when coupled with a mammoth publicity campaign, resulted in heavy sales most of which would otherwise have gone to Moulton Bicycles Limited.

Duff Hart-Davis' test of the 'RSW 16' involved a ride of some 40 miles from his Oxfordshire home to his office in London. This took him 3¼ hours and he concluded that the 'RSW', though tough, neat and well equipped, was heavier, less comfortable and needed more effort to propel than the Moulton. Nor did it adjust adequately to suit his 6ft. 2ins. frame. The cycling press also tested the 'RSW 16' against the Moulton and found it considerably slower.

The 'Ayrshire Post' of 6th August 1965 compared the two bicycles and commented on the 'RSW's' ponderous steering, poorer braking and soft saddle which yielded when the rider was pedalling. The Scottish Reviewer concluded that some women might prefer the 'situp and beg' riding position of the Raleigh but obviously preferred the Moulton himself.

The only alternative to the standard 'RSW 16' which Raleigh marketed was the 'Compact' car boot version which incorporated a 'shot-gun' folding action in the main beam of the frame and folding handlebars. This was intended to compete with the Moulton 'Stowaway' but comparatively few were produced. A moped called the Raleigh 'Wisp' was based on the fixed frame version of the 'RSW'.

The 'RSW 16' succeeded in giving a reasonably smooth ride. Over isolated bumps it was less successful than the Moulton but was actually slightly better on lightly pitted road surfaces. However, it was no long distance or speed machine.

Other manufacturers were also producing rival small-wheelers by the mid-1960's. Most of these were based on the use of an open frame with spannerless seat and handlebar adjustment and made use of 20" wheels, usually with semi-balloon tyres. Such bicycles included the Dawes 'Kingpin' and 'Newpin' and the Royal Enfield 'Revelation'. A few rigid framed machines with 16" x 1 3/8" tyres were manufactured and these included the Coventry-Eagle and Halford's 'Nimbus'. Later Raleigh produced the 'Triumph 20' on which the present Raleigh 20 and its variants are based.

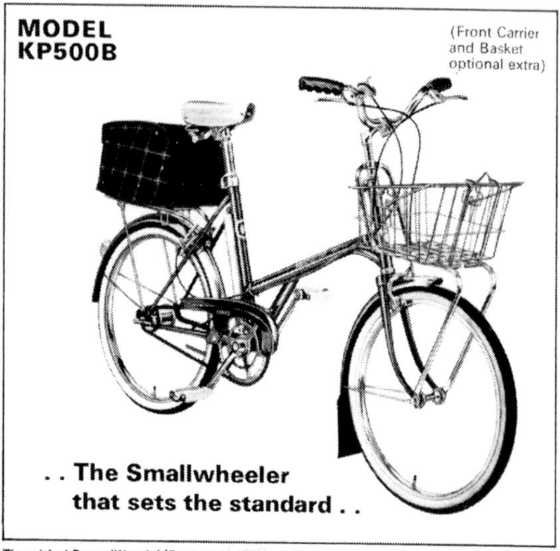

The original Dawes 'Kingpin' (From a mid 1960's catalogue, courtesy of Dawes Cycles Ltd.).

Such bicycles, though practical as utility machines, are inevitably a compromise and sacrifice either comfort or ease of propulsion (or both) when compared with the Moulton design. The majority of 20" wheel bicycles were, and still are, of fixed frame design although most makers offer folding or collapsible versions.

Small-wheelers also became popular on the Continent but most of these were folding bicycles with an open 'U' frame incorporating a hinge ahead of the bottom bracket. These machines usually have 20" semi-balloon tyres and are now frequently marketed in Britain via chain-stores and magazine advertisements. However, in the 1960's these foreign bicycles were almost unknown in this country.

In 1965 a 'toy' Moulton appeared. This was made under licence by Lines Brothers and sold as the 'Triang Junior 1970'. It had 14" x 1 3/8" tyres, ball -bearing hubs and working rear suspension.

In fact in 1965 potential Moulton purchasers had the widest range of options in the history of the machine. No fewer than ten versions of the full size Moulton were available ranging from the single speed 'Continental' to the 'Speedsix' club model and the custom-built 'S' range models.

In 1966 the smaller Moulton 'Mini' was introduced. This had 14" wheels and like the 'RSW 16', a shorter wheelbase. The 'Mini' was aimed at riders from the age of 7 up to and including smaller adults, particularly women. Later the same year the 'Mini Automatic' was announced. This was fitted with the Fichtel and Sachs two speed semi-automatic hub gear and back pedalling brake unit, which Moultons had first used in the 'Stowaway'. The 'Mini Automatic', which came complete with holdall, prop stand and dynamo lighting, was very much in competition with the Raleigh mini-bike.

At this time the motor racing champion Jack Brabham was signed up to promote the Moulton 'Mini' range. The campaign slogan was "Geoff Brabham rides a Moulton 'Mini' and so does his famous father".

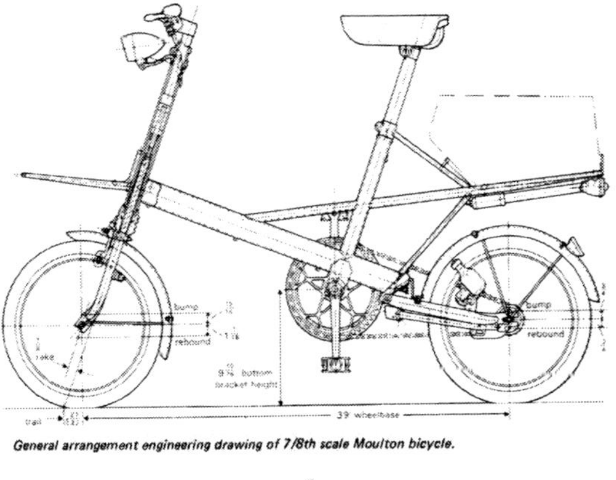

General arrangement engineering drawing of 7/8th scale Moulton bicycle.

The 'Mini Automatic' – in direct competition with the RSW 16 and one of the best interpretations of the 7/8th scale Moulton. (Photo courtesy of The Design Council).

By the time of the 1966 London Cycle and Motor Cycle Show, competition from other makers had forced some contraction of the Moulton range. Gone were the 'Standard', the 'Safari' and the 'Continental' together with its short-lived successor, the 'Automatic'. However, the new custom-built short wheelbase 'S Speed' made its debut at the Show and this was later ridden by Vic Nicholson when breaking the 'new route' Cardiff–London record. Also shown for the first time was the 'Mini Stowaway' although this was never actually marketed.

A year after Raleigh launched the 'RSW 16' the British Motor Corporation took over full control of all home and export production of the Moulton bicycle. Their subsidiary, Fisher and Ludlow, had been making Moultons for the home market at Kirkby, Liverpool since 1963 but only under licence. By 1966 a trade war with Raleigh was anticipated and BMC apparently intended to produce 100,000 Moultons a year. However, the combination of increasing competition and dealer resistance was destined to reduce this ambitious target somewhat.

We have already examined the competition but why the dealer resistance? Had not the Moulton saved the cycle dealers from a recession and created a new market in utility cycles?

The turnabout was caused, as much as anything, by the suspension and by the poor quality of the Kirkby built machines. If ridden in a normal manner, and if the simple instructions provided with the bicycle were complied with, the Moulton's suspension was relatively trouble-free, but if the bicycle was thoroughly abused damage could result. On the other hand the 'RSW 16' could be ridden up and down pavement curbs with relative impunity. Many bicycle dealers began to prefer the quiet life which resulted from concentrating their sales expertise on machines without the 'nuisance' of suspension.

To fuel any prejudice against the Moulton there had been a recall as a result of faults in the manufacture of the front forks. These were sub-contracted out to a specialist fork maker and some 11,000 defective units were produced. The fault was such that it could not be readily detected without destroying the forks. Most bicycles suspected of having faulty front forks were traced and the suspect part replaced free of charge but some defective machines may have slipped through the net; a point to bear in mind if contemplating purchase of an early Moulton[3]. Moultons developed a severe fork test to overcome the problem and thereafter no significant fork defects were reported other than those caused by abuse.

There were also some problems with certain 'Series One' rear suspension units which resulted from a changeover to carbon dioxide shield welding at the Kirkby BMC plant where the frames were built. Overheating caused undercutting during the welding which led to eventual fracturing of the trailing arm forks.

Moulton Bicycles soon became conscious of the fact that the 'Series One' rear suspension did not stand up well to abuse and the 'New Look' or 'Series Two' frame, introduced in 1965, incorporated much stronger, straight finned, pressed steel forks in lieu of the original curved and tapered design with brazed-in fork ends. This new suspension unit resulted in the bicycle sitting ¾" higher off the ground over the rear axle, thus giving slightly steeper tube angles.

It should not be assumed that doing away with suspension units would have solved any problems of frame or fork failures. Such defects are by no means uncommon in conventional machines[4]. Indeed, when Raleigh produced certain 14" wheel versions of the Moulton without front suspension this resulted in cracking of the frame around the junction of the head tube and main beam. A recall was then necessary in order to fit a special reinforcing bracket[5]. No such defect was recorded on Moultons fitted with front suspension.

As early as November 1963 Reyner Banham, in an article entitled "A Grid on two Farthings", had concluded that all small-wheeled bicycles would be referred to as Moultons. To some extent this prophecy came true and the technical mediocrity of many rival products reflected badly on the real Moulton. Anyone who tried out an 'RSW 16' believing it to be similar to a Moulton would be unlikely to be over-impressed.

The last catalogue produced by Moulton Bicycles Limited whilst still a part of the Fisher-Bendix Division of B.M.C. was an impressive large format full colour production featuring four models, the 16" wheel 'Deluxe' and three variants of the 14" wheel Moulton. A romantic theme was adopted based on 'heart' designs and slogans such as 'Moulton is for the young at heart'.

By the summer of 1967 production of the Moulton had reduced to about 750 units a week. Unconfirmed rumours suggested that the company was losing approximately £1,200 a week. At the same time, despite the apparent commercial success of the 'RSW 16', Raleigh's turnover and profits dropped by 8%. During this period Dr. Moulton's attention was turning back to automotive suspension design and to his development of the Moulton Coach. In his own words he 'providently decided to sell out before being totally submerged' by the competition from manufacturers of cheaper and inferior small-wheeled bicycles.

Two very similar financial offers were made for Moulton Bicycles Limited. One of the bidders was Raleigh and, as Dr. Moulton had originally intended that they should produce his bicycle, and because they were the largest cycle manufacturer in the world, an important decision was made.

In August 1967 Moulton Bicycles Limited became part of TI-Raleigh Limited of Nottingham.

Notes

1). David Duffield was Moulton Bicycles Limited's first Marketing Manager and now runs the Bicycle section of the Halfords chain of stores. A well known name in British cycling circles, he broke the Land's End to John O'Groats tricycle record in 1960 completing 872 miles in 2 days 10 hours 58 minutes. David owns a specially built Moulton 'MkIII' and still attends the Moulton Bicycle Club's Annual Meet. He was the subject of a cartoon in 'Sporting Cyclist' at the time of the Moulton launch which speculated that he might attempt the 'End-to-End' (Land's End to John O'Groats) on an apochryphal Moulton tricycle!

2). Alex Moulton's chapter on his suspension systems in 'Use of Rubber in Engineering' (see Chapter 2, Additional Reading C).) states that the rolling resistance of the 16" x 2" tyre at 35 p.s.i. is 50% higher than that of his 17" x 1¼" tyre at 70 p.s.i. Comparative rates for the suspension as against the balloon tyres are also given. (In crude terms the lower the rate the softer the ride). For the 'Series Two' Moulton the front rate is quoted at 72 lb.f/in. and the rear at 127 lb.f/in. whereas the RSW 16 tyre in a rigid frame gives a rate of 460 lb.f/in. to both wheels.

3). A reasonably indicative test to identify these 'rogue' front forks is as follows:

   a). Lift the bottom of the rubber bellows on the front suspension unit.

   b). With a small sharp instrument (e.g. penknife or compass point) scratch at the very base of the steering splines where they junction with the crown of the forks.

   If a 'gold' colour (indicating the presence of the brass used in brazing) is revealed the forks are likely to have been correctly manufactured. The test should be repeated at a number of points around the splines/fork crown junction.

   In an article on bicycle defects which appeared in the U.S. magazine 'Bicycling' in February 1979, Dr. David Wilson referred to the Moulton front fork failures and strongly urged owners of bikes with frame numbers lower than K.64.29 bought outside the U.K. to ensure that the original front forks have been replaced.

4). See 'Bicycles', an article in 'Which' May 1975, Consumers Association, p. 144.

5). It is believed that this bracket is still available from Raleigh. It is a crude and ugly but apparently effective device in two halves which are simply bolted together either side of the steering head tube/main beam junction. The finish is black with a white 'flash' motif, applied as an attempt to lighten the appearance.

Additional Reading – Primary Sources

A). 'Bold Attack on Diamond Frame' Cycling, 7th November 1962. This article describes the construction of the 'Series One' Moulton and gives a detailed specification of the prototype 'Deluxe' (Illustrated).

B). 'Lightweight Man'. 'The Versatile Moulton' Cycling, 14th November 1962. This article gives 'First impressions of the revolutionary bicycle'. (Illustrated).

C). 'Impact' Editorial of Cycling, 7th November 1962, the week of the Moulton launch at the Cycle Show.

D). See Chapter 2, Additional Reading E). particularly pages 45, 46 and 47. Combines subjective testing of a prototype Moulton 'Deluxe' with laboratory testing of the suspension system (Illustrated).

Secondary Sources

E). 'Spending Money on Things to Change your Life in 1963' Queen, Vol. 222, No. 5507. This includes a brief description of the Moulton from a fashion-conscious point of view.

F). Reyner Banham. 'A Grid on Two Farthings' New Statesman, 1st November 1963. An article describing the social impact of the Moulton.

G). 'Fashion on the Move' Sunday Times, 16th February 1964. A photo-feature reflecting the social acceptability of Moulton cycling in the mid 1960's.

H). JAK. Moulton cartoon Evening Standard, 10th November 1964.

I). 'The Easily Ridden Moulton Bicycle' Road Safety, October/November 1965. This article evaluates the Moulton design with regard to safety in use.

J). Duff Hart-Davis, 'Comment' – 'Enjoy London by Mini-Bike' Sunday Telegraph, 10th December 1967. This describes Moulton riding in the Metropolis (Illustrated).

K). Duff Hart-Davis. 'Mini-Bike Madness' Sunday Telegraph, 18th July 1965. Road testing the RSW 16. (Illustrated).

L). R.L. 'A New Era in Cycling' Ayrshire Post, 6th August 1965. This contains an article comparing the Moulton and the RSW 16. (Illustrated).

M). 'Evolution of the Moulton' Engineering, 1st July 1966. Describes the thinking behind the Moulton Mini range and briefly records the first four years of Moulton Bicycles Limited. Contains some interesting illustrations.

N). Engineering, 17th December 1965, p. 800. Reports the launch of the Triang Junior 1970, built under Moulton licence.

O). Design, No. 210, July 1966, Design Council, London. This contains an article on the introduction of the Moulton Mini range and discusses the ergonomics of widely adjustable small wheelers.

P). Bicycle Show cartoon spread Sporting Cyclist, December 1962. Includes the David Duffield cartoon referred to in Note 1). above.

Q). 'Challenge on Two Wheels' TR Journal, Winter 1964–5, Telephone Rentals pp. 23–27. The Moulton story in outline up to the end of 1964. Good illustrations including photographs of the Kirkby factory in action.

R). 'Bicycle Evolution' Design and Components in Engineering c. 1963. This magazine contained an article giving road impressions of the Moulton.

S). 'Raleigh to Gobble up Moulton to get Mini-Bike it Rejected' Daily Telegraph, 3rd August 1967. News item on "Blundered 'invitation to a merger' announcement".

T). 'Raleigh Buys Moulton – for an unknown price' Daily Telegraph, 8th August 1967. News item on the official announcement of the takeover.

U). Dr. Alex Moulton, CBE, RDI. 'Innovation' Offprint from the Journal of the Royal Society of Arts giving the text of an address by Dr. Moulton on the problems associated with innovative design. This covers his work on automotive suspension design, the Moulton bicycle and the Moulton coach together with some autobiographical and historical information of relevance to the general theme. (Illustrated).

V) Dr. David Gordon Wilson. Article in 'Bicycling' magazine (U.S.) on bicycle defects. Date unknown.

CHAPTER 4

RALEIGH AND AFTER

Raleigh are often portrayed as the villains of the piece as far as the history of the Moulton bicycle is concerned. Many people believe that they only bought Moulton Bicycles Limited to kill the machine off. Another story, repeated in at least one major book on cycling, is that as soon as Raleigh took over production of the Moulton, they dispensed with the 'complications' of suspension. Both views of the aftermath of the takeover are false.

When the takeover was announced Leslie Roberts, the Chairman of Raleigh, admitted that they were wrong to reject the original Moulton design. Poor market research was blamed for the fateful decision. However, the combination of Alex Moulton's 'inventive genius' and Raleigh's 'unparalleled resources' would be 'unbeatable' said the Chairman. The precise financial details entailed in the merger were never disclosed but, under the terms of the agreement, Dr. Moulton was retained by Raleigh as a consultant.

For three years after they acquired the Moulton Bicycle Company, Raleigh marketed both the 'Series Two' 16" wheel Moulton and the 7/8th scale 14" wheel version. Two versions of the larger machine were offered, these being the 'Major Deluxe' which corresponded to the last version of the 'Deluxe' made at Kirkby, and the 'Major' which was basically a reintroduced 'Standard'. Hence the range of full-size Moultons was actually increased by Raleigh, as the only 'Series Two' model marketed immediately before the takeover was the 'Deluxe'.

Raleigh continued the Moulton move away from brazed and riveted construction to edge brazing only which had begun with the introduction of the Moulton 'Mini'. The first 'Series Two' frames made at Kirkby differed from late 'Series One's' only by virtue of their redesigned rear forks and by the use of plastic cable guides in lieu of the original brazed on wire loops. 'Series Two' frames by Raleigh, on the other hand, featured a cross-bar brazed to the main beam where previously rivets had been used and the head tube was now edge brazed to the main beam. Furthermore the rear carrier strut and tie were brazed to the frame (and finished in the main frame colour) rather than screwed and bolted on. The rear carrier itself now plugged into the carrier beam at its junction with the carrier strut and tie, a detail similar to that employed in the 'Stowaway' M5 and in the '4 Speed' exported to Canada.

Another change of detailing came later with the use of pressed front forks rather than the better looking (and allegedly 'livelier') original pattern with brazed-in fork ends. Also the seat tube base was 'flattened' in such a way that viewed from the side it tapered down from the cross-bar to the bottom bracket.

It is widely thought that most of these modifications were originated by Raleigh but as early as 1965 a display model was produced at Bradford-on-Avon using these techniques (apart from the pressed forks). This bicycle, bearing the unusual frame-number 65 = 1 = 3, later passed into private ownership and is still in use.

The range of 14" wheel Moultons manufactured by Raleigh included the 'Mini' (later sold without front suspension) the 'Mini Deluxe', the 'Super 4', the 'Minx' (a three speed version introduced in 1969 to replace the 'Super 4', Sturmey Archer having ceased production of the F.W. four speed hub in 1968) and the 'Midi', another version of the 14" wheel Moulton with no front suspension. Both the Moultons which Raleigh sold without front suspension were subject to cracking of the frame around the junction of the main beam and head tube. As late as 1977 recalls were still in progress and a special strengthening plate was produced to overcome the problem. (See Note 5). to Chapter 3).

Examination of Raleigh sales literature circulated to the retail cycle trade reveals that they pushed sales of the Moulton quite hard. Their sales literature for public consumption was expensively produced, closely following the pattern of the last Moulton colour brochures produced by BMC. Raleigh's 1970 colour brochure for the Moulton was entitled 'Procreation' and illustrated the 'Major Deluxe', 'Major', 'Mini', 'Mini Deluxe' and 'Midi' models.

Later the same year came a bombshell, the simultaneous launch of three new bicycles by Raleigh in a blaze of publicity. These were the 'RSW Mk.III' – 'The Dolly One', 'The Chopper' – 'The Hot One', and the 'Moulton Mk.III' – 'The Smooth One'. Unfortunately the outlandish 'Chopper', more a toy than a real bicycle, caught most of the limelight and hence the launch of the 'Moulton Mk.III' was less spectacular than it should have been.

Moulton 'Minx' by Raleigh – a three speed version of the original 'Mini' and successor of the 'Super 4'.

Moulton 'Mk III' by Raleigh. (From Raleigh brochure).

Moulton '20' – prototype 20" wheel bicycle with rear suspension.

The 'Moulton Mk.III' was a very interesting machine and is described in more detail in the chapter entitled 'Variations'. As previously stated Dr. Moulton was retained by Raleigh as a consultant after the takeover and he designed the 'Mk.III' at their request. In fact a number of prototype Moultons were made at Bradford-on-Avon for Raleigh including several versions which, at Raleigh's instigation, had no front suspension. There was even a 'Moulton 20' which resembled a cross between a 'Raleigh 20' and a 'Moulton Mk.III'.

The 'Moulton Mk.III' was marketed in one version only and incorporated a completely new triangulated rear suspension assembly with a detachable rear carrier. The wheelbase and seat tube heights were reduced and the bike was fitted with a three speed Sturmey-Archer gear with integral cable operated hub brake. This machine has been the basis of a number of fine high performance conversion projects.

A modified prototype 'Mk.III', the 'Marathon' was ridden from England to Australia in 1970 as described in the chapter entitled 'On Safari'. Alex Moulton produced a limited number of 'Mk.III' prototypes which were equipped with 1¼" high pressure tyres and lightweight components and these were well received by the cycling press. Daved Sanders has a converted

'Mk.III' fitted with a Sturmey Archer five speed gear with which he regularly tours the Continent, including the Swiss Alps.

After its introduction the 'Mk.III' was the only full-size Moulton made by Raleigh. Its production run lasted for four years and by 1974 Raleigh had ceased to manufacture the Moulton bicycle in any form, although they apparently still possess the necessary manufacturing equipment.

In fact Raleigh produced the Moulton for some seven years of its eleven year total production run. Accurate production figures are very difficult to obtain but it would appear that the total number of Moultons produced at Bradford-on-Avon, Kirkby and Nottingham, and including those made by licensed overseas producers, was in excess of a quarter of a million which gives an average of around 500 units a week for 11 years.

Why then did Raleigh cease production? There seem to be three main reasons. Dealer resistance was one which, as commented on in the previous chapter, had started to creep in before the Raleigh takeover. Another reason was the bad name which small-wheeled bicycles had earned, largely as a result of the poor performance of rival products such as the 'RSW 16'. The third reason seems to lie in the fact that Raleigh is a large company within an even larger organisation making everything from electric cookers to house lintels. In such a company the opinions of accountants often hold sway over those of engineers. For instance, in the early 1970's Raleigh won a design award for a new self-adjusting brake for utility bicycles. After a couple of years this device disappeared, presumably because ordinary brakes are cheaper to manufacture.

In 1974 the market for bicycles was buoyant. It was a seller's market and Raleigh could sell as many machines as they could make. There was no economic reason to diversify their product and consequently both the Moulton and its pale shadow the 'RSW' were deleted from the range. Small wheel production was concentrated on the 'Raleigh 20' and it variants.

Alex Moulton's 1967 consultancy agreement with Raleigh was originally intended to last for 15 years but in 1975 the Nottingham Company terminated the arrangement (using its half-term option) in order to concentrate on 'in-house' design. Thereby Raleigh denied themselves any future involvement with the innovations and evolutionary work of Alex Moulton. It is interesting to contrast subsequent fashion-orientated Raleigh products (such as the 1981 'Bomber' with its 26 x 2.125" tyres) with the Moulton philosophy of technical improvement in bicycle design.

The Moulton featured in 'Design' magazine's quarter century review of the best of British Industrial Design (June 1977). In the text Peter Knottley describes the bike as 'the first real advance in bicycle design for 50 years'. (Reproduced courtesy of The Design Council).

What then is the legacy of the Moulton? The very existence of adult small-wheeled and collapsible bicycles as we know them is almost entirely due to the influence of the Moulton. Yet no currently produced small-wheeler compares with the Moulton for versatility. None is suitable for serious touring and none has been successfully raced against conventional lightweights.

The Bickerton 'Portable', with its 14" front and 16" rear unsprung wheels, is an ingenious folding bicycle which is lighter, and folds smaller than the Moulton 'Stowaway'. However, it is extremely uncomfortable over rough surfaces and very prone to whip. The 'Micro' is another folding model which incorporates narrow section 16" wheels. It is less compact and heavier than the Bickerton but similarly uncomfortable. (It also features a Moulton-type plastic chainwheel guard).

Most small-wheeled bicycles today use a 20" wheel and are a compromise between conventional large-wheeled machines and the Moulton. Because of the lack of suspension these bicycles are generally less comfortable than even their big-wheeled brethren. Sometimes semi-balloon tyres are fitted to help mitigate this problem but this only results in increased rolling resistance. The majority of these bicycles are also remarkably heavy. Dawes make great play of the lightness of their 'King-pin' small-wheeler yet is weighs roughly the same as the prototype Moulton 'Deluxe' despite its lack of suspension. Most small wheelers weigh more, the 'Raleigh 20' being around 38 lbs.

Few small-wheelers can carry luggage as well as could the Moulton. The carriers are usually flimsier and narrower, and where front carriers are fitted, these are usually fixed to the front forks, thus adversely affecting the steering when laden. Only in 1980 did Raleigh introduce a frame fixed front carrier for the latest '20 Shopper', 18 years after Alex Moulton incorporated the idea into his design.

Nevertheless the 20" wheel machines are popular and serviceable for urban use and for short shopping trips. They invariably incorporate the unisex, 'Instant' adjustment features pioneered by the Moulton. The 'Raleigh 20' and its variants, sold at various times under the Triumph, BSA, Sun, Humber, Sunbeam, Phillips, and Hercules trademarks, was the Nottingham company's biggest selling design as late as 1977. It still sells well and is one of the better currently produced small-wheelers. However, as one who has owned two big-wheelers, four Moultons and two 20" wheel bicycles, I can confirm that the 'Raleigh 20' does not compare very favourably with the Moulton.

Will the Moulton ever return? In April 1977 'Cycling' carried an article by Peter Knottley which disclosed that Dr. Moulton was intending to produce a new 'Super-Tourist' model and an up-market commuter bike. At that time the tourist model was intended to be built of Reynolds 531 tubing and to incorporate an even more advanced suspension system, 17" x 1¼" nylon high pressure tyres, 12 speed Derailleur and superlative luggage capacity. The pump was to be hidden in the seat tube and the whole ensemble capable of being rapidly packed away into a small carrying bag. Mark Ottaway's article in the 'Sunday Times' of 30th March 1980 also stated that Alex Moulton had designed a new Moulton bicycle and in fact it is now certain that a new version of the machine will be manufactured at Bradford-on-Avon although precise details are shrouded in secrecy. Production is scheduled to commence in 1983. This bicycle will be sold as an 'Alex Moulton' because the original 'Moulton' trademark belongs to Raleigh. It is intended that the 'Alex Moulton' will be produced in limited numbers for the more discerning section of the bicycle market.

After Raleigh withdrew the Moulton in 1974 a rumour circulated that they were going to relaunch it with solid tyres as the 'Puncture Proof Bike'. Indeed, John Woodburn, who broke the Cardiff-London record on the Moulton in 1962, always felt that utility versions of the bicycle should be developed for use with solid tyres. Alex Moulton did experiment with solid tyres but they were rejected because of various problems including poorer roadholding, poor wet grip, higher rolling weight and difficulty in renewing tyres.

In the meantime many people still remember the Moulton with affection and two bodies exist which, in their own ways, are helping to ensure that the name lives on.

Moulton Preservation was founded by Michael Woolf and Helen Marsland and aims to link owners who wish to preserve their machines. It also endeavours to locate Moultons in good condition for preservation and wrecks for cannibalisation. Moulton Preservation aims to offer technical advice and to attempt restoration of Moulton Bicycles at its London address.

The Moulton Bicycle Club is run by Jim Poslett (previously Daved Sanders) under the Presidency of Dr. Moulton himself. The club organises events including an annual run and also publishes a news magazine. For the addresses of both organisations see the Appendix.

The existence of these two organisations will help to ensure that the Moulton lives on and news of the new 'Alex Moulton' bicycle is very heartening to devotees. Soon after I bought my first Moulton a school-teacher (and complete stranger) approached me and said that she admired the Moulton because it showed that people were still thinking. It is encouraging to know that in 1981 Dr. Moulton is 'still thinking'. And, as 'Cycle Trade News' put it in February 1981 'Whatever happens from now on the inventiveness, perception and steadfastness of Alex Moulton should not be forgotten: All of us in the trade and industry are in his debt . . . .'

Note

1). A photograph exists of a Raleigh-type 'Series Two' Moulton equipped with a Moulton child seat (lacking the back rest shown elsewhere as part of this accessory) but also fitted with a carrier similar to that used on the MkIII. This machine, which appears to have had 1 5/8" tyres and a front wheel hub brake, is actually badged-up as a 'Moulton Series 3' (not to be confused with the Mk.III) and is thought to have been a prototype for production by Raleigh in South Africa. Other equipment included a rear wheel rim dynamo (with headlamp fitted half-way down the head tube) and a short reach handle-bar stem.

Additional Reading – Secondary Sources

A). Peter Knottley. 'Big Enjoyment from Two Small Wheels' Cycling, 16th April 1977. Describes evolutionary work on the new 'Alex Moulton' bicycle. (Illustrated).

B). 'Moulton. Was it Really a Magic Name? And What Actually Happened . . . . .? Cycle Trade News, February 1981. This gives a concise history of the Moulton. Some of the information on Moulton variants and their prices is slightly inaccurate.

C). Stephen Dallaway. 'Moulton by Raleigh' Cycletouring, October 1970. Reviews the production model 'MkIII' (Illustrated).

D). Motor Cycle and Cycle Trader, 2nd June 1970 p.49. Contains a detailed specification of the 'MkIII' complete with 'Talking Points for Dealers'. Also contains the specifications of the simultaneously launched 'RSW MkIII' and 'Chopper'. (Illustrated).

E). Daved Sanders. 'MkIII Special by Paul Godolphin' Moulton Cyclist, Issue No. 13, Autumn 1980. Describes a very fine conversion of a production 'MkIII' into a high performance racing machine.

F). Peter Knottley. 'Testing a New Moulton' Cycletouring, February/March 1970. An interesting account of a 1000 mile road test of a lightweight prototype 'MkIII' built of Reynolds 531 tubing. (Illustrated).

G). Peter Knottley. 'The Moulton Prototype' Bicycling! (U.S.A.), February 1970.

H). Peter Knottley. 'Look – It's Peter's new Moulton!' Cycling, 27th March 1971.

I). 'The Smooth One' Raleigh brochure for the introduction of the MkIII, Summer 1970. Folds out to form wall-chart.

J). '25 year Review 1952–1977' Design, No. 342, June 1977, p.55. This review of the best of British design includes the Moulton bicycle with comment by Peter Notley (sic). (Illustrated).

K). Richard Stevens. 'Bike Fantastic' Design No. 302, February 1974 pp 54–61. 'Musclepower visions from the Japanese bicycle design competition' A very well illustrated article which demonstrates the ongoing influence of Moulton's ideas particularly in the Danish design on p.57.

L). Michael Strutt. 'Some New Angles on the Bicycle' Financial Times, 13th January 1979, p 17. This article discusses the present state of the bicycle industry with special reference to innovative design. Mention is made of the original Moulton and its effects as well as the proposed new machine. The Wilson–Willkie recumbent machine (see Note 2). to Chapter 2) is also described (Illustrated).

M). See Chapter 3, Additional Reading T).

CHAPTER 5

MOULTON SPEED

In the issue of 'Cycling' magazine for 12th December 1962 a full page advertisement placed by the newly formed Moulton Bicycles Limited announced 'Long Distance Speed Success'. John Woodburn, a rider on loan from Ted Gerrard Cycles, had broken the Road Racing Association Cardiff to London record by just over 18½ minutes riding one of the new small-wheeled bicycles.

The Moulton advertisement pointed out that 'each model in the Moulton Bicycle range has the identical frame and suspension to that used on the record breaking ride'. This was obviously a great propaganda coup. Everyone likes to be associated with a winner and racing success would obviously help sales of the new bicycle. More to the point, Woodburn's success demonstrated that any power losses through the suspension system or through higher wheel bearing friction were inconsequential.

Breaking the Cardiff–London record was the culmination of weeks of preparation by the Bradford-on-Avon team, under the inspired leadership of David Duffield, himself a record breaking cyclist. Arthur Wright reported on the test riding programme in the December 1962 edition of 'Sporting Cyclist' and made the point that all the Moulton team, from draughtsman to marketing manager were cyclists, Alex Moulton himself being a member of the Cyclists Touring Club.

Arthur Wright commented on the lively steering of the Moulton but pointed out that this was also a characteristic of a good lightweight bicycle which one soon got used to. The machine which Woodburn was riding at the time had a 68 tooth chainwheel driving a Sturmey-Archer AC close ratio hub to give 94, 101 and 107" gears. This necessitated use of a special 11 tooth sprocket which was produced by Moulton's Technical Manager Phil Uncles, (who was closely associated with development of the Moulton bicycle) and his machine shop boss John Clinton.

The test course used by the Bradford-on-Avon team consisted of five miles of undulating public road, marked off in half-mile lengths. On the day

John Woodburn in training on the Moulton 'Speed'.

Arthur Wright visited The Hall, John Woodburn rode the course both ways using an aerodynamic cowling, in 21 minutes 53.6 seconds, at an average speed in excess of 27 miles per hour (In fact on the return run his average speed exceeded 30 miles per hour). This was just one of a large number of test runs and Woodburn was actually riding the equivalent of four time-trials a week during this period. He had also closely approached his 1959 record of 57 minutes 33 seconds for the Bristol South '25' course over the Bridgwater Flats. He took just 12 seconds longer to ride the course on the Moulton (this time without the cowling). In the 'Sporting Cyclist' article Woodburn was reported as saying that, even without the aerodynamic fairing the Moulton was at least as fast as a conventional machine.

At the time of the Cardiff–London record success John Woodburn was the National Independent Pursuit Champion. He first made an attempt on the Cardiff–London run for Moultons on 15th November 1962 but it was abandoned after 83 miles which he had covered in 3 hours 35 minutes. This meant that he was 10 minutes behind schedule to beat the existing record held by C.M. Caton since 1957.

Everything seemed to go wrong on the first attempt. Woodburn was prevented from starting his ride for half an hour by a gear fault and eventually commenced his attempt on a spare Moulton which was undergeared for his style of riding. After 38 miles he was able to switch to his own machine but then got caught up in rush hour traffic in Cardiff and Newport. Then on the London side of Newport he injured his right knee in a fall while negotiating road works. Nevertheless he carried on, despite the problems and the lack of any significant following wind, but eventually, when all real hope of breaking the record had gone, he gave up near Northleach. At the time 'Cycling' reported that the result 'as far as the potentialities of the machine are concerned, are quite inconclusive'.

Less than a month later, John Woodburn tried again and this time it was a very different story. George Pearson wrote a full page article on the ride in 'Cycling' under the banner headline 'National Record on the Moulton'. This time everything had gone to plan and in fact the timekeeper, E.R.Wilkinson, only just got to Marble Arch (the final destination) in time to record the success.

Although attempting to break long distance cycling records in December is almost unheard of, the weather was good on 9th December 1962. Woodburn started well covering 25 miles in the first hour but in the second hour he dropped to 21 miles. The third hour resulted in a mileage of just under 23 miles and the fourth, which included climbing the worst of the Cotswold Hills, gave just over 25 miles.

For the first half of his ride he had to fight hard to keep up to his schedule which aimed at a 12 minute improvement on C.M.Caton's 1957 record. It is rumoured that, by the time he reached the Oxford Bypass, Alex Moulton had dragooned Alec Issigonis, the inventor of the Mini, out of a hostelry in order to view Woodburn race by on the Moulton 'Speed'. By the time Woodburn reached Wheatley he was on schedule and in the fifth and sixth hours he achieved 23.9 and 22.4 miles per hour respectively. The last 18 miles were covered in 43½ minutes making a total of 162 miles in 6 hours 43 minutes 29 seconds at an average speed of approximately 24 miles per hour.

Rider and machine appeared to labour most on the hill climbs and George Pearson noted that Woodburn admitted to being only a moderate climber. Pearson felt that possibly the Moulton fell in the same category. On the other hand it was noted that Woodburn's skills lay mainly in pushing a big gear on the flat and downhill and on the descent into High Wycombe 50 miles per hour was achieved.

John Woodburn breaking the Cardiff—London record on the Moulton 'Speed' in 1962 — Note the hub gear trigger. (Photo courtesy of 'Cycling').

So it was that Alex Moulton gained the prestige of a speed achievement to more or less coincide with the launch of his revolutionary bicycle. Originally he had contemplated a 25 mile ride which was how John Woodburn, Short Distance Amateur Champion of 1961 came to be involved. Later a 50 mile attempt was contemplated before the final decision was made to try the Cardiff–London run. Consequently Woodburn was riding beyond his optimum distance. On the other hand the Cardiff-London record was 'relatively unexploited' as 'Cycling' put it. Nonetheless, as George Pearson said, the Moulton was 'a goer' and this ride proved that it would 'get you there without any loss of power'.

The machine ridden by Woodburn for the record breaking ride had a standard Moulton frame with the carrier beam sawn off behind the seat tube and naturally equipped with racing saddle and drop handlebars. As many lightweight components as possible were fitted including a T.A. cotterless crank set with 7 1/8" cranks and Dunlop sprint wheel rims with 16 x 1¼" No. 5 tubular tyres. The front wheel had 16 spokes whilst the rear had 20. The transmission consisted of a 64 tooth chainwheel with the tiny Moulton-produced 11 tooth sprocket and the variable gear was again a hub unit rather than the customary derailleur mechanism generally fitted to racing machines.

The main reason for the use of a hub gear was the fact that no derailleur block with a small enough sprocket was available at the time. The gear selected was a Sturmey-Archer F.C. four speed close ratio unit which is no longer in production. John Woodburn had not used this gear before but recollects experiencing no problems with it and he appears to have quite liked it.

Most hub gears work on the epicyclic principle which involves a sun wheel (a small cog on the wheel axle) meshing with, and surrounded by, planet wheels (also small cogs, usually three in number) which in turn mesh with an internally toothed gear ring. By various clutching arrangements each epicyclic gear train can give up to three ratios; an upward shift, a downward shift and direct drive. Hence the familiar three speed hub gears marketed by Sturmey-Archer, Shimano, Puch and Fichtel & Sachs all contain single epicyclic gear trains.

If a second set of sun and planet wheels of different proportions is incorporated into the gear the possibility of another three gears is offered but, as one of these will also be direct drive, the net total will be five gears. Before the Second World War Sturmey-Archer produced the AF gear which

was used for the 100,000 miles in 500 days record according to Hugh Blackeby of 'Cycling World'. Although this gear was a twin epicyclic type, the fifth gear was sacrificed in favour of obtaining four speeds on one control lever. An experimental five speed Sturmey-Archer hub was in use during the War but the company decided to 'keep it up their sleeve' until a later date. Hence in the immediate post-war period they launched the FW, FM and FC hubs, being four speed wide, medium and close ratio gears respectively.
The S5 five speed was not launched until the 1966 London Cycle and Motor Cycle Show. This hub, the only one of its type in the world, employs two changers; one acting like a normal three-speed, the other as an overdrive and underdrive to give 'super high' and 'super low' gears. Jack Lauterwasser[1], who eventually became one of Moulton's engineers, long ago evolved a technique for converting four speed hubs into five speeds, thus liberating the 'repressed' super high gear.

Many of the mass produced Moultons were fitted with the F.W. wide ratio four speed but for Woodburn's ride the close ratio F.C. gear was used and this was geared to give a very high top of 104" with a lowest gear of 70" compared with a top gear of 81" on the Moulton 'Standard'. The original Moulton 'Speed' ridden by John Woodburn is in Dr. Moulton's private collection and a replica can be seen in the National Motor Museum at Beaulieu, Hampshire.

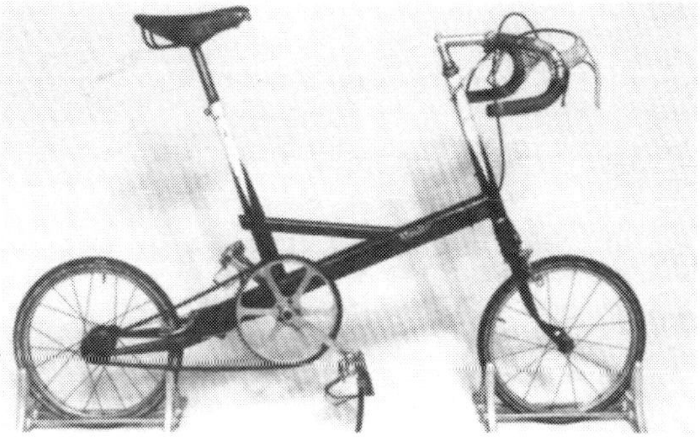

John Woodburn's Moulton 'Speed' on which he broke the Cardiff–London record in 1962.

About 18 years after his famous ride I asked John Woodburn for his reminiscences of the Moulton as a racing machine. He pointed out that the version he rode was a very unrefined 'gas pipe' version and remembers the machine as being very good downhill, especially over rough surfaces, because of the excellent road-holding of the rear suspension. He was not so happy about its hill climbing especially when the rider was 'honking' or standing on the pedals out of the saddle. Woodburn felt that the front suspension was unnecessary and undesirable as he felt it tended to waste power. Alex Moulton, on the other hand, maintained that the rider should stay in the saddle, use the gears and adopt the rotary style of riding recommended in the cycling text books[2].

John Woodburn was very keen on the rear suspension though and scotched the myth which circulates in some racing circles that the rear suspension gave a kick coming out of corners, resulting in a loss of control. In fact Woodburn found no problems in cornering on the Moulton.

Although he is not a devotee of ultra short wheelbase bicycles, John Woodburn did consider that the original Moulton's wheelbase was too long. Despite such reservations he still has some affection for the machine and is proud of the RRA Yearbook entry for December 1962 where it states that he broke a record on a new type of bicycle.

Woodburn considers that the Moulton was potentially faster than a conventional machine for time trialling on the flat and definitely faster downhill, especially over rough surfaces. He also considers that it was invincible in four man pursuit because of the better slip-streaming allowed by the smaller front wheel.

This is an interesting point. At Easter 1963 'Cycling' published a photograph of a four man team on Moultons. This team, A. Millard, M. Ives, A. Collins and C. Groom all of Coventry gained an outright team victory over a Leicestershire team on conventional machines at the Butts Stadium, Coventry on 11th April 1963. Furthermore, when Alex Moulton was negotiating with the Huffman Manufacturing Company in order to arrange U.S. manufacture of the Moulton under licence, he took two track racing Moultons with him. He asked the somewhat sceptical Huffman executives to select four equally strong and experienced riders, none of whom had ridden a Moulton before, and arranged a 2000 metre pursuit race with two conventional lightweight track machines against the two Moultons at Encino Velodrome, Los Angeles in March 1965. The riders on the small-wheelers won.

The Moulton four man pursuit team pedal to victory at Coventry – Easter 1963.

The 1963 sprung track version of the Moulton 'Speed'.

Before the Cardiff–London ride John Woodburn had been involved with the 'Cowl', one of Alex Moulton's experiments with streamlined fairings fitted to a racing Moulton. This cowling was built to Alex Moulton's design by a student engineer, Ralph Street, who felt that such devices could save two to three minutes in a 25 mile race. The first version consisted of blue doped linen on a wire frame and was later followed by a glass-fibre unit. Fitting the fairing to the Moulton was easy (on the first version two wingnuts were used) and the small wheels permitted full-lock steering to be retained. Arthur Wright reported on these experiments in his 'Sporting Cyclist' article and noted Woodburn's observation of the strangeness of riding in 'still air' with the wind pushing past outside and hearing all the transmission noise normally drowned out by the wind. However, such fairings are not permitted under Road Racing Association Rules and Alex Moulton was concerned about rider safety in cross-winds, so the experiments were eventually discontinued. The original 'cowls' are preserved in the Moulton Museum.

John Woodburn experiments with the 'Cowl' – 1962. Note the tail tube still in position.

A year after he broke the Cardiff–London record Woodburn was scheduled to attempt the London–York run for Moultons but illness forced him to abandon the attempt and thereafter he returned to conventional cycle racing. His record on the Moulton still stands. Shortly after it was established the Severn Bridge opened and since then all Cardiff–London runs have been conducted on a route approximately ten miles shorter than that ridden by Woodburn.

At Easter 1963 the late Tom Simpson, arguably Britain's greatest post-war racing cyclist, tested the track Moulton on the Herne Hill circuit in South London. He was sufficiently impressed to tell Alex Moulton that he would be pleased to race on the small-wheeler 'next week' were he not already under contract to Peugeot. Simpson's testing of the Moulton is commemorated in a Portland Stone bas-relief plaque, sculpted in 1974 by Barry Baldwin, which adorns the stonework of the Moulton factory at Bradford-on-Avon.

The next major rider to take up the Moulton was Reg Randall[3]. He already held the 'End-to-End' record (Land's End to John O'Groats) on a conventional machine and felt that he could improve on his time by riding the Moulton. He made two attempts using a Moulton 'Speed' on the 18th August and 8th September 1964. Unfortunately, on both occasions the wind drastically changed direction about half way up the route and both attempts were eventually abandoned. Nonetheless, the hourly timings up to the time the wind changed were very creditable and both attempts were taken seriously in the cycle racing world. Reg Randall's 'Speed', on which some 440 miles were covered in 24 hours, is housed in Dr. Moulton's Private Museum.

After Reg Randall came Vic Nicholson who was to achieve considerable success in time trials riding a Moulton 'Speedsix'. In 1965 he won 15 major time trials and was placed in 9 others. His success with the Moulton included a 25 mile time trial (Solihull C.C. Invitation) on 23rd May which he completed in 56 minutes 32 seconds, a 50 mile time trial (Wessex Road Club) on 13th June completed in 1 hour 58 minutes 53 seconds, and a 12 hour event (Western T.T.A.) on 15th August during which he rode 252¼ miles. Vic Nicholson was also successful in track events coming first in the 1965 Reading Track League Pursuit Championship.

Although John Woodburn's Cardiff–London record still technically stands he was not the only Moulton rider to break a record between these two cities. After the opening of the Severn Bridge a rider on a conventional machine set up a new record on the shorter route. On 3rd September 1967 Vic Nicholson, riding a Moulton 'S Speed' shattered the record by a further 17 minutes 44 seconds. This was just after the announcement of the Raleigh takeover. Only a fortnight earlier Nicholson had broken the Midlands RRA Birmingham–Bristol–Birmingham record by 25 minutes 13 seconds.

The machine used for these rides was prepared by the 'S' unit at Bradford-on-Avon and made use of the special Reynolds 531 Lightweight Moulton frame set which was first made available in 1966. This consisted of a new frame, front and rear forks complete with suspension units, head fittings and seat pillar, and weighed just 9½ lbs. A racing machine based on this frame set and fully equipped complete with double chainwheel weighed about 24 lbs. (By comparison, the lightest current Dawes racing bike weighs 22 lbs.). The 'S' Speed frame set cost 24 guineas when introduced. A few fully assembled 'S' Speeds were made to order and sold for around £80. The model was introduced at the 1966 London 'Cyclex' where it was shown with a massive 72/64 tooth chainwheel. It was the first short-wheelbase full-size Moulton (40").

Vic Nicholson at Pencoed on the 'Speedsix' during the W.C.A. '25' Championship c. 1965. (Photo courtesy of 'Cycling' and R.V. Good).

Vic Nicholson's 12 speed '531' Moulton 'S' Speed, complete with 74 tooth chainwheel. Another Cardiff—London record breaker.

Apart from the 'S' Speed, two true sports models were featured in the catalogues circulated by the Bradford-on-Avon Company. When the new bicycle was introduced in 1963 it was intended to produce a 'Speed' (M4) retailing at £39 19s. 6d. This was fitted with sprint wheels, tubular tyres, airlite hubs, G.B. alloy 'Maes' bars, stem and coureur brakes, alloy mudguards, Brooks or Unica saddle and detachable rear carrier.

The rear suspension was fitted with twin adjustable friction dampers and the transmission consisted of Milremo 5 pin cranks with a 64 tooth T.A. chain-ring driving a 12 or 14 tooth sprocket to give fixed gears of 86 or 73. As an extra a Sturmey-Archer AC 3-speed close ratio gear could be fitted to give gears of 79-86-92 or alternatively the FC 4-speed close ratio could be supplied to give 64-77-86-93. The frame colours were white or bright red.

However, this machine was never actually marketed and the 'Speed' (M4) as offered to the public was merely a sportier version of the Moulton 'Standard'. Autumn 1965 saw the arival of a true lightweight speed machine in the Moulton range. This was the 'Speedsix' (M6). 'Cycling' magazine reviewed this bicycle under the headline 'We're convinced – you will be too' (11th September 1965). Their reporter, (Ken Evans, later editor of 'Cycling') actually rode the machine from Bradford-on-Avon to London and back. He wrote 'The steering, although it was lighter than normal owing to the small wheels, was easy to handle, even when "honking". On this model, both the front and rear suspension has been stiffened to counteract the "bouncing" effect obtained on the utility models, whilst still giving a far smoother ride than normal . . . . . The way is now clear for any club or racing man to change to the Moulton system and still have a machine as capable and responsive as his much-loved lightweight'.

'Cycle Touring' (Oct.–Nov. 1966) also reviewed the 'Speedsix'. Their reviewer thought it was a touring machine 'par excellence' but did not feel it was a vast improvement in lightweight design. Nonetheless he conceded that it was 'a very likeable and interesting machine fully deserving an equal place beside the traditional mount'.

The 'Speedsix' weighed 28 lb. when fully equipped with carrier and mudguards, and cost 38 guineas. It featured a completely detachable rear carrier and beam, and was probably the first mass produced bicycle in the U.K. to be fitted with a 6 speed derailleur. This was a Moulton modified Cyclo Benelux P2 gear (based on a Campagnolo design). The block was designed by Moultons and incorporated an 11 tooth smallest sprocket (later Moulton blocks were to feature an incredibly small 9 tooth sprocket). The

Moulton speedsix!

Dressed for travel

Just replace the mudguards and rear carrier, add a front carrier (optional extra), and your Moulton Speedsix is perfectly dressed for the road — with all the carrying capacity you could possibly need. And with Moulton's unique suspension system, the new Dunlop H.P. tyres give practically the same rolling resistance as tubulars, without loss of comfort even over the roughest going. That's Moulton universality! A truly superb bicycle with proven competition performance, equally suitable for distance riding and touring. So if you take your sport seriously enough to want two or three machines, the Moulton Speedsix is the *one* bicycle for you!

The greatest range, the master design **Moulton**

Moulton speedsix!

Stripped for action

SPECIFICATION INCLUDES COMPLETELY DETACHABLE REAR CARRIER & BEAM, WHICH CONVERTS BICYCLE FOR RACING REQUIREMENTS. 6-SPEED GEARS 48.5/56.5/63.7/72.8/78.4/92.7 INCORPORATING SPECIALLY DESIGNED Moulton **CYCLO** P2 GEAR. UNIVERSAL FRAME TO SUIT RIDERS OF ALL AGES. UNIQUE Moulton RUBBER SUSPENSION SYSTEM WITH REAR DAMPER. SPECIAL **DUNLOP** H.P. TYRES ON ALLOY RIMS. **TA**60 ALLOY CHAIN RING WITH 555 CRANKS. ALLOY **GB** MAES BARS ON 3½ ALLOY STEM. NARROW-SECTION LIGHT ALLOY GUARDS. **BALILLA** ALLOY BRAKES INCORPORATING QUICK-RELEASE MECHANISM. SPECIAL SPORTS BUTT LEATHER SADDLE BY **MIDDLEMORES** LTD. **T. D. CROSS** HEAD & BOTTOM BRACKET FITTING AND MANY OTHER QUALITY COMPONENTS. COLOURS: YELLOW, AND LIGHT BLUE. THE RECOMMENDED RETAIL PRICE: 38 GNS INCLUDING TAX

The greatest range, the master design **Moulton**

Two facets of the Moulton 'Speedsix' — from Moulton brochure.

gear mechanism was hung from a bracket brazed onto the rear fork several inches ahead of the back axle thus giving maximum chain wrap-round and better ground clearance. The ratios thus offered were 48.5/56.5/63.7/72.8/78.4 and 92.7.

The rear suspension was fitted with twin friction dampers and the wheels had a new improved design Dunlop High Pressure 17 x 1¼" tyre[4] on Dunlop steel rims with Milremo alloy hubs. (Later machines had Milremo alloy rims). The brakes were Balilla Corsa 59 side pulls and the alloy handlebars and 3¾" stem were by G.B. A T.A. 60 tooth alloy chainring with 555 cranks and Phillips racing pedals were fitted, and the saddle was a special butt-leather type with extra long adjustable carriage by Middlemores. Alloy mudguards and a 12" pump completed the specification and the 'Speedsix' was available in pale-blue or yellow.

Some 'Speedsixes' were modified to take a front changer. The thicker than normal oval section seat tube meant that a conventional fitting could not be attached. One solution, used by the specialist firm Hinds, was to braze a small piece of tubing onto the top of the main beam behind the seat tube. A conventional changer mechanism could then be fitted.

The sporting cyclist's desire to toughen up the Moulton's suspension was recognised in the 'Speedsix' because, apart from the fitting of rear dampers a harder rubber mix was employed. Prior to that toughening up of the front suspension had sometimes been achieved by shortening the rubber column and coil spring and/or packing out with extra hollow steel spring abutments. It appears that this was not officially approved practice as far as the designer was concerned. For the production 'Speedsix' both the rubber column and the spring abutment were slightly longer than on the utility Moultons.

In fact, an experimental track racing Moulton without suspension exists. It incorporated unorthodox inverted drop handlebars to reduce stem length and save weight and was built in 1968. Fully equipped the machine weighed just 16 lbs. Unsprung Moultons were used for four man pursuit racing in Canada against conventional track machines. The riders in both teams were carefully matched. Invariably the Moultons were first past the post.

When raced against conventional machines the Moulton tended to generate ill-feeling amongst the other riders. Fears of riding up over the small rear wheel were voiced and the big-wheelers disliked the superior slip-streaming ability and quick steering of the Moulton. It was not Alex Moulton's intention to generate unpleasant feelings in racing circles and it was decided to let like race against like as a 'contest between athletes' rather than machines. Consequently, Moultons did not pursue track racing to any great extent, preferring to concentrate on longer distance solo record attempts and time trials.

In any case the Moulton was primarily intended as a multi-role bicycle; a cyclist's system capable of use for delivering newspapers, commuting to the station, riding to Australia or winning time trials, using fundamentally the same frame and suspension design. The fact that it could be successfully raced, even in its most primitive form, demonstrated the validity of the design. It is significant that no other small-wheeler has successfully challenged the classic, diamond frame, lightweight bicycle's domination of cycle racing.

Nor should it be thought that the era of the high speed Moulton is dead. Despite the shortage of machines and parts, especially 1¼" high pressure tyres, and the fact that no Moulton racing bicycle has been commercially available for fourteen years, devotees still maintain the 'Speed' tradition.

The unsprung track Moulton produced in 1968. It weighed just 16 lbs.

In 1978 Daved Sanders took part in the Paris to Harrogate Centenary Ride on his modified Moulton 'Mk. III'. He was the only entrant to ride a Moulton and of 108 starters only 32 completed the ride, including Daved. This run involved covering 800 kilometres in 53 hours with little or no sleep.

Daved Sander's machine has an absolutely standard Raleigh produced Moulton 'Mk.III' frame but incorporates front forks from a 'Series Two' bicycle. The original steel chainwheel and cranks were retained but the wheels were replaced and alloy rimmed 17" x 1¼" wheels with Dunlop high pressure tyres fitted instead. The five-speed gear is the S5 Sturmey-Archer hub unit which has been modified to operate via ratcheted, derailleur type handlebar plug levers. Alloy drop bars and brakes, racing saddle and metal pedals complete the re-equipping of this Moulton which is regularly used for Continental touring, including the Swiss Alps.

Using this bicycle Daved also successfully completed the Windsor–Chester–Windsor Brevet ride in June 1977 during which, despite appalling weather and a slower riding companion, he completed 375 miles in 40 hours. And in the summer of 1981, Vic Nicholson once again mounted a Moulton and rode the Bristol South '25' winners reunion race.

12 speed transmission of a lightweight 'Mk III' special. It features a Moulton designed 6 speed block with a tiny 9 tooth sprocket. (Photo by author).

Vic Nicholson riding a 'Mk III' special at the Bristol South '25' winners reunion in 1981 — note the centre-pull brakes. (Photo courtesy of 'Cycling').

Notes

1). Jack Lauterwasser is a name well known to the older generation of cyclists. He rode for Britain in the 1928 Olympics, gave his name to a style of handlebars and created the 'Lauterweight' racing bicycle, now a collectors item. He also worked for Rudge-Whitworth and for Sturmey-Archer where he acquired his unparalleled knowledge of hub gear technology. In the 1950's he designed and built an open frame light-weight big-wheeler.

Later he joined Moulton Bicycles Limited where one of his specialities was the 'S' range of custom-built Moultons. Now retired, Jack continues to take an interest in the Moulton and still tours regularly. His son Alan was formerly Sales Manager for Moulton Bicycles and now runs the Peugeot Bicycle operation in the U.K. (For details of Jack's five-speed conversions see the Appendix).

2). A rumour still circulates that the suspension of Woodburn's machine was 'locked up solid' for the Cardiff to London record ride. I put no credence in this tale for a number of very good reasons. Firstly, as Arthur Wright put it, Alex Moulton watched over Woodburn 'like the trainer of a Thousand Guineas candidate' and would have been the first to notice if his carefully nurtured suspension system was not working (which, apart from anything else, is quite obvious when the rider mounts or dismounts the machine). Then again Wright reported that, whilst following Woodburn on the 10 mile test course, he could plainly see the action of the rear suspension. Remember also that Woodburn approved of the rear suspension because of its superior roadholding qualities. So apart from tightening up the friction dampers for race conditions it is hard to envisage any other modification having been made to the rear suspension.

It is known that John Woodburn eventually disagreed with Alex Moulton over the front suspension characteristics and it is possible that, unknown to the inventor, someone uprated the front suspension (which was later official Moulton policy for the racing versions of the bike) though I have no evidence that this was actually the case. Even if it were it is a far cry from 'locking up solid'. It should also be borne in mind that Woodburn's front wheel was a tubular-shod 16" alloy rimmed sprint with just 16 spokes. If it had been unsprung could it have made it from Cardiff to London at record breaking speed on public roads with John Woodburn in the saddle? Even if the wheel did not buckle, the bicycle would have been very difficult to control and fatiguing to ride. Momentum losses caused by impact with road surface irregularities would also have been much greater.

3). R.F. Randall also held the 1000 mile record which he broke in 1960 with a time of 2 days 10 hours 40 minutes.

4). The development of the High Pressure 17 x 1¼" tyre was the result of close collaboration between Alex Moulton and the Dunlop Tyre specialists at Fort Dunlop.

Additional Reading – Primary Sources

A). George Pearson. 'National Record on the Moulton' Cycling, 12th December 1962, p.10. A full description of Woodburn's record breaking ride. (Illustrated).

B). Arthur Wright. 'What's Awheel for the Future?' Sporting Cyclist, December 1962, pp.31–34. An interesting account of the early test-riding programme of the Moulton 'Speed'. (Illustrated).

– Secondary Sources

C). 'Woodburn Abandons Record Attempt' Cycling, 21st November 1962. News item on first Cardiff–London attempt.

D). Keith Thorrington. 'Technitopics – Moulton's Speedsix' Cycle Touring, October–November 1966. Road testing the 'Speedsix'. (Illustrated).

E). K.E. 'We're Convinced – You Will be Too' Cycling, 11th September 1965. Road tests the 'Speedsix' and gives detailed specification. (Illustrated).

F). 'Technitopics – Personal Touch' Cycle Touring, June–July 1965. Describes two high quality customised 'Speedsixes' (one for a disabled rider) produced by W. Hinds Ltd. of Ealing. (Illustrated).

G). 'Nicholson's Best in 12-Hour Race' Bristol Evening Post, 17th August 1965. An account of Vic Nicholson's victory in the Western Time Trials Association's 12 hour event.

H). 'Then and Now – A Nostalgic Look at the Past Winners of the Bristol South '25' Who Met Again Recently' Cycling, 6th June 1981, inside back cover. Photo-feature which includes Vic Nicholson on the 'Speedsix' in 1965 and on Des Isley's 'Mk III Special' in 1981.

I). Alex Moulton. 'Alex Moulton Takes a Futuristic Look at Cycling' Cycling, 21st November 1965, p.10. The inventor's thoughts on possible future developments in cycling including comments on the role of the Moulton in cycle racing (Illustrated).

J). Daved Sanders. 'Windsor–Chester–Windsor Brevet Ride – 600 km in 40 hours Riding a Moulton Bicycle' (Privately published).

K). Daved Sanders. 'Paris–Harrogate Centenary Ride – 800 km in 53 hours Riding a Moulton Bicycle' (Privately published).

L). See Chapter 4, Additional Reading E). for a description of a 'Mk III Special'.

M). 'Vic (on a Moulton) Knocks 18 Minutes Off' Cycling, 9th September 1967. Describes Nicholson's successful attempt on the Cardiff–London 'New Route' record.

CHAPTER 6

ON SAFARI

In his 1973 book 'The Bicycle', R. John Way of the Cyclists' Touring Club stated that the Moulton was a practical touring bicycle and that 're-equipped with first-class fittings, the Moulton, with its low centre of gravity, would become an excellent carrier for heavy loads.'

In fact the Moulton was first put to the test as a tourer back in 1962 even before it was publicly launched. The cycling illustrator Brian Walker and his wife Rosemary toured the inhospitable terrain of Western Iceland on a pair of Moulton 'Safaris' and random excerpts from their journal were printed in two successive centre page spreads in 'Cycling' in November 1962. Bearing in mind the fact that the only paved roads in Iceland are in the capital, Reykjavik, this was obviously as good a test as any for the new machine.

Brian Walker commented that the roads were 'merely tracks varying in texture from a well-trodden beach to a badly kept rockery with ruts formed by high ridges of stones and gravel, making us thankful for the suspension on our bikes.' The 'capacious bags' of the 'Safari' were obviously appreciated as was the bike's ability to glide over rough terrain whilst a party of riders on conventional lightweights floundered on the loose rock surface.

The Moulton 'Safari', (M3) produced between 1963 and 1966, was the most expensive model in the standard range at around 41 gns.[1]. It was specifically aimed at the touring cyclist and was supplied with a good quality leather saddle, the Brooks B17 Narrow Champion (later the B15). Alloy components included the mudguards, G.B. Maes handlebars and stem, and Coureur side-pull brakes. Early versions had a T.A. chainring with Milremo 5 pin cranks whereas later models had a 54 tooth Williams C34 chainset with 6¾" cranks. A Sturmey-Archer F.W. four speed wide ratio hub was fitted, with the option of a two speed derailleur converter for an extra £3 which would then give a choice of eight speeds. The gears were very slightly lower than those of the Moulton 'Standard' being 41–50–63 and 80" on the four speed version. The two speed derailleur converter, introduced in Autumn 1963, was originally by Gian Robert and later by Cyclo Benelux. It used 13 and 15 tooth sprockets to give 38–46–57–72/44–53–66–84" gears.

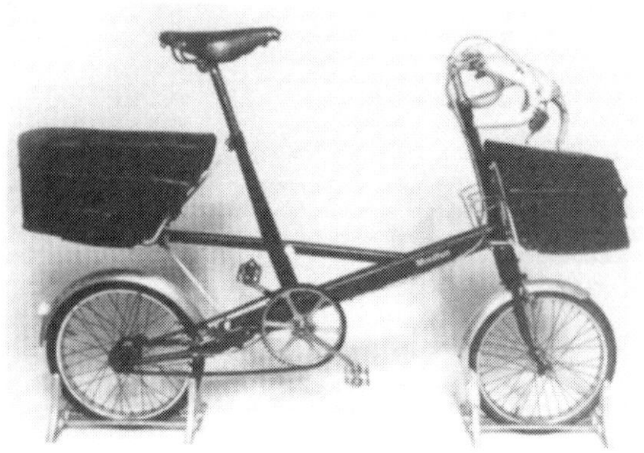

The Moulton 'Safari'.

Twin carriers were fitted as standard, thus enabling 20 lbs. of luggage to be carried up front and 50 lbs. behind. (These payloads were common to all 'Series One and Two' Moultons). Both carriers were fitted with the superior quality 'Safari' holdalls, the rear bag incorporating useful side pockets.

The M3 'Safari' was equipped with the regular 16 x 1 3/8" size tyres and steel rimmed wheels. The front hub was by Airlite and earlier versions of the bicycle had the amber walled 1 3/8" Sprite tyres fitted rather than the all black utility version. The machine also boasted twin bottles and carriers. Early 'Safaris' were also fitted with 'C' spanner-adjustable friction dampers to the rear suspension pivots.

The eight speed version of the 'Safari' weighed 41 lb. fully equipped for touring and originally you could buy a 'Safari' finished in either silver grey or olive green. Later the silver grey option was deleted. A non-catalogued blue 'Safari' was also produced. The Science Museum was presented with a 'Safari' by Alex Moulton and this machine was displayed as the latest stage in the evolution of the bicycle[2].

The Moulton 'Safari S' and 'Speedsix'. The prop stands shown were not included in the specifications.

For 1965 the new 'S' range of Moulton bicycles was announced. These were handmade at Bradford-on-Avon under the supervision of Jack Lauterwasser and represented the highest specifications attainable for the 'Deluxe', 'Stowaway' and 'Safari' models. The MS3 'Safari S' cost £54. 19s. 6d. when introduced and featured sleeved G.B. alloy Tourmalet handlebars, Balilla alloy brakes (with levers bolted onto the bars), a choice of Brooks Champion or Nitor saddle, a light alloy detachable rear carrier, B.H. Airlite hubs, double-sided Lyotard alloy pedals and all cables concealed within the frame. Bluemels 'Club' plastic mudguards were fitted, as was a special front fork spoke lock. A pair of Coloral bottles and cages were also supplied. Vertical drop out rear forks and special gear attachment were provided to accommodate the Cyclo P2 Gear with Moulton six speed block. (This version of the P2 had the cage hanging in more or less the usual way, not 'backwards' as on the 'Speedsix'). The 'Safari S' weighed about 30 lbs. without its bags (about the same as the current Dawes 'Super Galaxy' tourer).

The gears thus offered were 35–48–61–70–77 and 84, 33–41–51–61–71–83 or 43–51–57–66–71 and 83. Alloy rimmed 1¼" wheels were fitted complete with Dunlop high pressure tyres. Otherwise the specification was the same as that of the M3 'Safari'. The 'S' version was available in polychromatic gold or holly green.

So much for the specifications but what was the 'Safari' like to ride? In November 1963 'Cycling's' 'Nimrod' reviewed the standard version and headed his article 'Comfort on the Moulton Safari M3'. He found that, contrary to his expectations, it 'seemed to be on rails as I tried it out around wet, greasy corners.'

'Nimrod' found the carriers and their rigidly attached bags ideal and noted that 'any additional weight tends to make the machine more stable, rather than top-heavy as with an ordinary bicycle.' Unlike many Moulton reviewers, he found that braking in the wet required care, not because of any worries over wheels skidding but because he felt the rims took a long time to dry out. 'Nimrod' also commented on the need to modify the "honking" technique on a Moulton but concluded that he liked the bicycle and was looking forward to riding it further.

However, it was not really necessary to own a Moulton 'Safari' to enjoy touring Moulton-style. Any well-maintained Moulton could be adapted to make a good tourer, especially if fitted with a sports saddle, metal pedals and toe-clips. My own tours were carried out on a Moulton 'Speed' (the M4 production model, not the racing machine). This already had a Middlemores leather saddle, down-turned allrounder handlebars on a 3½" forward extension and steel pedals. As extras I fitted toe-clips, flint catchers and a front carrier with 'Safari' holdall.

On some tours I used the rear holdall provided with the 'Speed' but later abandoned this in favour of an army kit-bag held on with elastic straps. This proved a very satisfactory solution to the problem of carrying many bulky items, including a sleeping bag and cooking gear, in one easily transferable bag. This is particularly useful if the bicycle is to travel by train or ferry, remote from the cyclist. The rider of a conventional touring machine may well have to strip off two front panniers, a handlebar bag, two rear panniers, a saddle-bag and a loose sleeping bag wrapped in polythene before he can deposit his bicycle in the guard's van. A pair of good-sized holdalls are much easier to cope with! Furthermore the aerodynamic Moulton holdalls minimise wind resistance by presenting a reduced frontal area.

This apart though, what was the Moulton like as a touring machine? On my tours of the Continent, which took in parts of Belgium, France, Holland and West Germany, my travelling companions rode conventional machines varying from a sophisticated lightweight to a heavy roadster and so a subjective comparison with these machines can be made.

I experienced no significant problems with the Moulton whereas the rider of the lightweight fell off in the rain on the A.2, dented a wheel rim on a tram line in Brussels and buckled a wheel on a cycle track near Aachen. Another companion with a 'Chain Store' sports machine suffered no major defects but had continual minor problems including losing his chain outside the E.E.C. headquarters in Brussels. The rider of the roadster suffered few reliability problems but, his machine was slower and because of poor weight distribution and the 'sit up and beg' riding position of his machine, he actually managed to roll his mount backwards when starting off from traffic lights near Cologne. (He also had his front wheel stolen in Heidelberg High Street but that's another story!).

The Moulton could be ridden flat-out over Belgian paved roads where the riders of conventional machines had to slow right down. A light but firm control of the handlebars was required on such surfaces and the suspension made an excellent job of smoothing the ride, even with a heavy load of camping equipment on board. The strength of the 16" wheel was demonstrated by the fact that not the slightest dent was put into the rims nor was a single spoke broken.

The low-speed stability of the machine, allied to the suspension and well-thought-out gearing, enabled me to ride up the subsidence-damaged, stone-setted Black Forest inclines alongside my companions who were reduced to pushing their conventional bicycles. The descent to the Rhine Valley from Kniebis was made on good smooth surfaced roads with many a hairpin curve. The stability of the Moulton and the absence of speed wobble when heavily laden enabled me to leave my colleagues far behind and by the time they caught up with me, a mile or two further down the road, I had overtaken two German cyclists on lightweights and a Triumph Herald and had bought and half eaten a bar of chocolate! This exhilarating descent contrasted sharply with one I had made a few years earlier into Bath. That was on my big-wheeler and pannier-induced 'tail whip' had made that a rather disagreeable experience.

My own touring experiences pall into insignificance when compared with those of many Moulton tourists. For instance, in 1964 Tim Woodman rode his Moulton '4 Speed' right across Canada from Halifax, Nova Scotia to Tofini, Vancouver Island. The '4 Speed' was an export model produced at Bradford-on-Avon for sale in Canada, and was similar to the Moulton 'Standard'. Woodman's machine, now in Dr. Moulton's collection, had 'Safari' holdalls fitted to the front and rear carriers and a rim dynamo mounted on a reinforced mudguard stay (a Moulton accessory prior to the introduction of brazed-on dynamo brackets on the 'Series Two' rear forks).

Tim Woodman, a retired RAF Wing Commander, was fifty when he undertook his 4,600 mile ride. He had never previously undertaken a major cycle tour. His aim was to visit wartime Canadian friends whilst enjoying some of the varied landscapes of the North American continent. Consequently he proceeded at a leisurely pace, completing the transcontinental journey in 63 days. Nevertheless that is still an average of some 73 miles a day for two months – quite an achievement for a middle-aged rider with little touring experience and an indication of what could be achieved even on a utility version of the Moulton bicycle.

Prior to Tim Woodman's ride, Tony Keeling had ridden 8,000 miles from London to Teheran and back on a Moulton 'Standard'. Another, long distance rider was Peter Lea of Wigan who rode his 1966 'Safari S' 30,108 miles in 1967 alone. During his ownership of the machine he averaged 62.5 miles a day without a major breakdown. Daved Sanders, Honorary Secretary of the Moulton Bicycle Club, has also toured extensively on his modified 'Mk III' with lightweight fittings, 1¼" high pressure tyres and Sturmey-Archer S5 five speed hub. His tours have even included the Swiss Alps.

In September 1966 Mario P. Mitton, a handicapped cyclist, toured Portugal on a Hinds-customised 'Speedsix'. With him were Bob Naylor, also on a Moulton, and Clive Jerome on a conventional lightweight tourer. Mario's account of the tour was later printed in 'Cycletouring' where he stated that for comfort the Moulton was 'unbeatable'. His sensitive crippled left arm was never uncomfortable despite appalling road surfaces. However, he criticised the durability of the Dunlop high pressure tyres which though 'lively and good road-holders' tended to suffer from carcass weaknesses. The tyres were subsequently improved.

Another long distance Moulton cyclist was Mike Maughan who rode from London to Calcutta. Unfortunately, he crashed into a handcart loaded with steel reinforcing bars with disastrous results for his machine. Not surprisingly the account of his travels, published in 'Cycling and Sporting Cyclist', was entitled 'Trouble with Wheels on the Road to India'.

But perhaps the most famous of the Moulton tourists is Colin Martin who, in 1970, cycled to Australia. He was an experienced cyclist who had ridden conventional lightweights for some years and who had also acquired some racing experience. Colin intended to cycle round the world and he selected a Moulton for his epic journey because of its fully sprung and very strong wheels and its vast carrying capacity. He wrote to Bradford-on-Avon to enquire about certain modifications to the standard Moulton and the result was the 'Marathon', a one-off prototype 'Mk III' machine incorporating the original 'Stowaway' feature of a dividing main beam, thus enabling the bicycle to be disassembled for safe-keeping in an hotel room or for carriage as baggage on trains, boats or aircraft.

A recent round the world tour by Scandinavian cyclists was carried out on bicycles fitted with twenty speed gears. Proving that such excess is not strictly necessary. Colin had used the Fichtel and Sachs 'Torpedo-Duomatic' two speed semi-automatic hub gear with integral back-pedal brake. His top gear was 68" and his transmission system got him from Chippenham, Wiltshire to Kalgoorlie, Western Australia (where his bicycle was stolen) with no servicing other than weekly oiling. A double chainwheel without changer[3] was fitted thus enabling an overall raising or lowering of ratios to suit a particular terrain.

The only real problem encountered with the bicycle was the sagging of the rear carrier. This was repaired by a blacksmith en route and the design was subsequently modified for production model 'Mk III's'.

The Moulton 'Marathon' – before and after Colin Martin loaded up. Note the experimental carriers.

Colin Martin's tour is well described in the excellent little book 'Half-way Round' co-written with Peter Knottley but sadly now out of print. Another Moulton tourist (on a more modest scale) to have gone into print is the actress Eleanor Bron who published a book of reminiscences on the subject. Her Moulton was also stolen!

Despite being out of production for many years, Moultons are still in use for long distance touring; for instance in 1980 David and Joan Lester covered 1100 kms. in Hungary.

After his great trek Colin Martin stated that in his opinion the Moulton was the best touring bicycle in the world and that he would recommend it to any serious cycle tourist. There can hardly be a better recommendation.

Notes

1). The price gradually increased from £39 19s. 6d. to £43 19s. 6d.
2). The 'Safari' in the Science Museum has now been replaced by a Moulton 'Mk III'.
3). Twin sprockets were also fitted. With a well judged combination of double chainwheel and twin sprockets it is possible to manually realign the chain (without the necessity for a tensioning arm or for adjusting the length of the chain) and yet still maintain a 'true' chain line.

Additional Reading – Primary Sources

A). Brian and Rosemary Walker. 'Land of Wind and Fury' Cycling, 21st November 1962 pp. 14 & 15 and 28th November 1962 pp. 14 & 15. Two centre-page spreads describing the pre-launch Icelandic tour on prototype Moulton 'Safaris'. Illustrated with sketches by Brian Walker

B). 'Nimrod'. 'Comfort on the Moulton Safari M3' Cycling and Mopeds, 27th November 1963. Road tests the 'Safari' and gives a detailed specification. (Illustrated).

C). Colin Martin and Peter Knottley. 'Half-Way Round'. Formerly available from the CTC but now out of print. An interesting little book largely based on Colin Martin's journal during his ride to Australia (Illustrated).

– Secondary Sources

D). Mario P. Mitton. 'Small Wheels Sunwards' Cycletouring, February 1967. Describes a tour of Portugal on a modified 'Speedsix' (Illustrated).

E). Mike Maughan. 'Trouble with Wheels on the Road to India' Cycling and Sporting Cyclist, May 1969. Describes the later stages of a solo ride from London to Calcutta (Illustrated).

F). See Chapter 2 Additional Reading H) p. 23. Brief reference to the suitability of the Moulton for touring (Illustrated).

G). See Chapter 3 Additional Reading Q) pp.25–26. Brief reference to Tim Woodman's Canadian Tour.

H). Peter Knottley. 'Having Another Go' Cycling, 6th June 1970. Account of a short Easter tour on a Moulton in Cornwall. The author was accompanied by Colin Martin. (This was a few weeks before the latter set out for Australia).

I). Peter Knottley. 'A Mini-Tour on a Mini-Bike' Cycling, 7th March 1970

J). Peter Knottley. Three instalment account of the author's ride to Istanbul with Colin Martin on the first stage of the latter's ride to Australia. (The rest of the way Colin travelled solo) Cycling 10th, 17th and 24th October 1970 (Illustrated).

K). David and Joan Lester. 'Moultons among the Magyars' Moulton Cyclist, No. 14 Winter 1980. Account of a recent tour in Hungary.

L). 'Bron on a Bicycle makes a New Book' Sunday Telegraph Supplement, 8th October 1978. A review of Eleanor Bron's first book (Illustrated).

M). Eleanor Bron. 'Life and Other Punctures' Andre Deutsch 1978. The book itself but an 'Anecdotal Autobiography' rather than a book specifically for cyclists.

NB: Many of the items referred to in Chapter 5 – Additional Reading will be of interest to cycle tourists. 'Moulton Cyclist', the Moulton Bicycle Club Newsletter, also publishes accounts of Moulton tours from time to time.

CHAPTER 7

STOWAWAY

The idea of a collapsible bicycle was not entirely new when the Moulton 'Stowaway' M5 was launched. For instance, Peugeot had produced a folding bicycle for military use in 1898. Mikael Pedersen, the Danish-born creator of the legendary 'Dursley Pedersen', also produced a folding machine about the turn of the century. Another early folding bicycle was the 'Faun', a diamond frame 'safety' also produced in a lady's version. And B.S.A. produced military folding bicycles for both the First and Second World Wars. Nonetheless, when the 'Stowaway' was announced, it was a very novel machine. It was aimed at motorists, boat owners, caravanners and flat dwellers. Although the majority of Moultons were fixed frame models, the idea of the collapsible small-wheeler so caught the public imagination that many people thought all Moultons were car boot bicycles.

The 'Stowaway' in the modest sized boot of a Morris 1100 (itself equipped with Moulton hydrolastic suspension). (Courtesy of The Design Council).

The 'Series One' 'Stowaway' was fitted with the Perry Coaster B500 single speed back-pedal brake but 'Series Two' versions were equipped with the same semi-automatic two speed gear as the Moulton 'Automatic'. This hub also incorporated a back-pedal brake and was made in Germany by Fichtel and Sachs. In fact this was claimed to be the only non-British component used on the bicycle as it was always Moulton's policy to use British parts wherever possible.

The reason for the use of rear hubs incorporating coaster brakes was the fact that the main beam of the bicycle took apart completely and hence it was impracticable to have cables linking the two parts[1]. The same problem precluded the user of variable gears operated by cables, hence the use of the Fichtel and Sachs 'Torpedo-Duomatic' hub[2].

This gear, unlike the Sturmey-Archer hubs, works in direct drive in low gear thus giving maximum efficiency when hill climbing (with Sturmey-Archer three-speeds direct drive is given by second gear, whereas four and five-speeds give direct drive in third). To change gear the rider backpedals approximately a quarter of a revolution, and to brake, a half turn of the pedal is required.

A useful feature of this hub is that, when approaching a halt in top gear, the action of braking automatically engages low gear, ready to start off again. Other advantages of the 'Duomatic' include the absence of cables to stretch or break and the fact that the gear cannot go out of adjustment or slip. The automatic 'Stowaway' was supplied with gears of 47 and 63" but these could be raised or lowered, if required, by fitting a different sized sprocket.

Apart from the different rear hub and the fact that the frame could be dismantled, the only other major difference between the 'Standard' and 'Stowaway' M5 was the use of narrower handlebars to facilitate storage. The 'Stowaway' cost £26 19s. 6d. in its original 60" gear single speed version and the price increased to £29 19s. 6d. when the two speed gear was fitted. Later the price rose to 31 guineas. The frame was generally finished in polychromatic blue, although a non-catalogued pale grey version was also produced.

An 'S' range 'Stowaway' (MS5) was introduced for 1965 at £44 19s. 6d. and this incorporated as many lightweight fittings as possible. These included Dunlop 1¼" high pressure tyres on alloy rims, 17" flat alloy bars, G.B. alloy stem and Coureur front brake. Plastic mudguards were fitted and the seat pillar was made of alloy. A B.H. Airlite front hub, front fork spoke lock,

Williams AB77 alloy cotterless chainset, chrome chain cover and kick-down stand were all included in the specification. The Fichtel and Sachs 'Duomatic' two speed back-pedal hub was fitted and this gave ratios of 51" and 68" when driven from the 54 tooth chainwheel via an 18 tooth sprocket. The MS5 frame was fully chromed giving a very distinctive appearance.

Compared with some later collapsible bicycles the 'Stowaway' looked quite complicated to disassemble, there being five stages to the operation. First the rear carrier was removed by standing on the opposite side of the bicycle to the chain, holding the seat tube with the left hand and loosening the quick-release toggle immediately ahead of the carrier. The carrier was then slid out with the right hand (this left the thin carrier struts and half the carrier beam still attached to the frame, unlike the removable carriers on the 'Speedsix' or 'Safari S')[3]. Next the saddle and pillar were removed by slackening the seat height adjuster toggle.

The main frame was then 'attacked'. The spanner supplied with the 'Stowaway' incorporated an allen key and this was used to loosen the screw in the top of the main beam by two full turns. Then the 'cross bar' was held with the right hand whilst the left hand gripped the main beam. The index finger of the left hand was employed to depress the safety button under the main frame and with a 'steady movement' the two sections of the machine were separated.

Lastly the front wheel was gripped between the legs and the bolt head on top of the handlebar stem was slackened off with the spanner until the bolt protruded by about ¼" whereupon it was given a hard tap or two with the back of the spanner to ensure that it dropped thus releasing the cone and permitting the handlebars to be turned in an anti-clockwise direction until in line with the front wheel. Now all that was necessary was to pack the pieces away.

These instructions were very clearly outlined with the aid of diagrams and photographs in a folder produced by the makers and it was claimed that, with practice, the whole procedure could be carried out in 40 seconds. However, the idea of gripping the front wheel between the legs whilst releasing the handlebar stem with a spanner was all very well for the smartly suited gentleman shown in the instruction leaflet. He was obviously working with a clean, new bicycle in a photographic studio. Performing the same task whilst similarly clad, with a muddy, oily bicycle on a wet day, with perhaps an important business meeting a quarter of an hour away, would be a less attractive proposition. This, of course, is a problem which is to some extent common to all collapsible bicycles.

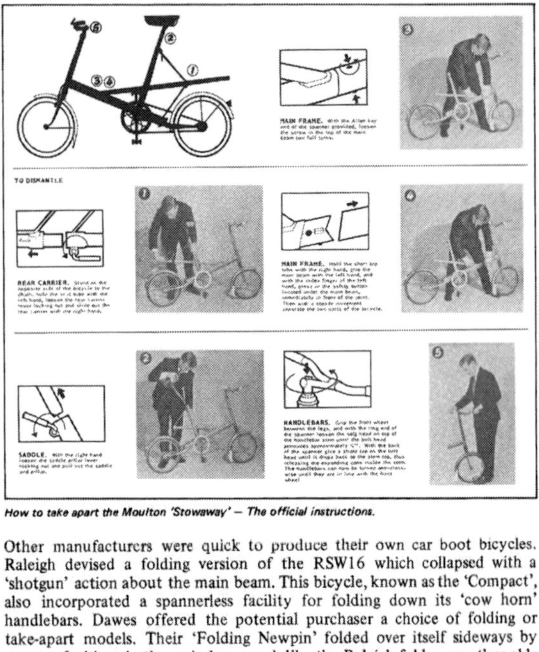

How to take apart the Moulton 'Stowaway' – The official instructions.

Other manufacturers were quick to produce their own car boot bicycles. Raleigh devised a folding version of the RSW16 which collapsed with a 'shotgun' action about the main beam. This bicycle, known as the 'Compact', also incorporated a spannerless facility for folding down its 'cow horn' handlebars. Dawes offered the potential purchaser a choice of folding or take-apart models. Their 'Folding Newpin' folded over itself sideways by means of a hinge in the main beam and, like the Raleigh folder, was thus able to incorporate a standard three-speed and rear brake. This model also incorporated spannerless handlebar adjustment. The 'Take-a-part Newpin' had a single speed back-pedal brake and a double prop stand thus enabling both hands to be left free to pack away the front section. Dawes claimed that this bicycle, which had no carrier, could be disassembled in 'two seconds' and packed into a space 34" x 28". (No third dimension was given). The Moulton 'Stowaway' on the other hand would fit into a container 42" x 28" x 14" which meant that it could fit into the boots of reasonably small cars such as the BMC 1100/1300 range.

The Norwegian licence-built version of the 'Stowaway' – South African Moultons also featured these large section 1 5/8" tyres.

By 1967 the original 'Stowaway' had been discontinued following rationalisation of the Moulton range. It was scheduled for replacement by the M9 based on the 7/8th scale 14" wheel Moulton frame. The M9 was similar in many ways to the 'Mini'. However, it retained the 'Duomatic' two-speed back-pedal brake of the later M5 'Stowaways', and was equipped with 6½" cranks and a suitable seat pillar for adult use. This was the only version of the 'Stowaway' to be catalogued with spannerless adjustment of the handlebars and, in common with some rival machines, no carrier was fitted. The machine was finished in Autumn gold.

The disassembling of the M9 was comparatively simple. The entire bicycle ahead of the seat tube and bottom bracket was removable. A curved plate linked the 'cross bar' with the main beam and at the base of this plate a pair of 'hooks' passed over the bottom bracket. The weight of the rider ensured that the curved plate rested against the seat tube and a locking ring around the seat tube dropped over the top of the curved plate and was screwed down by hand to lock the two sections of the frame together. The seat and handlebar adjusting toggles enabled the saddle and bars to be turned, dropped or removed as necessary. No tools were necessary to dismantle this 'Stowaway' and the makers claimed that it could be dismantled in 15 seconds. The M9 was announced at the 1966 London Cycle Show but never got beyond catalogue stage, plans for its production being curtailed by the Raleigh takeover.

Comparison of stow condition — classic lightweight versus Moulton. The 'Stowaway' shown here is a prototype lightweight 'Mk III', similar in many ways to the 'Marathon'.

After 1967 no collapsible Moulton was ever mass produced. The original 'Stowaway' mechanism was however reintroduced for the purpose-made Moulton 'Marathon', a version of the 'Mk.III' on which Colin Martin rode to Australia in 1970.

In later years many low priced European 'U' frame folding bicycles have been sold in this country, often via petrol stations, chain stores or magazine advertisements. Though the 'Stowaway' is no longer produced the market it created continues and some interesting designs have emerged such as the very lightweight and compact Bickerton 'Portable' but none has combined the smooth ride and easy pedalling of the Moulton. Actually you can still buy a 'Stowaway' but the machine which bears the name today is a folding version of the Raleigh 'Twenty'. Raleigh own all the old Moulton trademarks and could presumably rename the 'Chopper' the Moulton 'Speed' if they so desired (perish the thought!).

Although with the benefit of hindsight the Moulton 'Stowaway' was not the easiest collapsible bicycle to dismantle, the fact that the parts completely separated had certain advantages. It meant that instead of having to hump the whole bicycle into the car boot in one move, each part could be lifted and packed away in relative comfort. Also there were more options as to how the machine could be packed into a given space or spaces. The necessity of using a spanner to release the handlebars has some disadvantages but, on the other hand, this system did allow the owner to change to any style of bars that suited him and he never had to contend with the whip inherent in the handlebars of many flimsier collapsible machines.

The main beam joint of the M5 and MS5 appears to have been a successful engineering solution when compared with the crude and flimsy hinges seen on some folding bicycles[4]. After all, Colin Martin's 'Marathon' incorporated this feature and has anyone else ridden a collapsible bicycle from England to Australia?

Most important of all, though, the 'Stowaway' had all the major features of the Moulton design, the same wheels, suspension, luggage carrying capacity and race proven frame geometry. The 'Stowaway' was a collapsible version of a bicycle for the open road, rather than a machine designed merely to get the rider from the car park to the office.

Notes

1) In the 1970's Moultons developed a quick-release system for connecting control cables on machines employing the 'Stowaway' take-apart frame joint. Hence it is now technically possible to equip a Moulton 'Stowaway' with any cable operated brake and/or variable gear system.
2) The 'Duomatic' hub offers direct drive and a 36% increase in gearing. It weighs 1.1 kg. (2.4 lbs.) without sprocket. (For further details see Appendix E).
3) A pre-production 'Stowaway' prototype did incorporate a fully removable 'Speedsix' type carrier. This machine also had a more pronounced front fork rake in common with the 'Deluxe' prototype illustrated in 'Cycling' (7th November 1962).
4) It is strongly recommended that the 'Stowaway's' main beam joint be opened and lubricated monthly in order to prevent the mechanism from seizing. It is also important to ensure that the machine is never ridden with the joint slack as this can permanently damage the mechanism.

Additional Reading – Primary Sources

A) Geoffrey Hancock. 'The Automatic Stowaway' Motoring, February 1965. Two page illustrated feature.
B) Various catalogues and brochures produced by Moulton Bicycles Limited between 1963 and 1967.

– Secondary Sources

C) 'Moulton Bicycle – Servicing Data Sheet No. 11–2' (Trader Aids – Second Series) Motor Cycle and Cycle Trader 1965. Apart from much other useful information on the Moulton, this sheet includes an 'exploded' illustration of the 'Stowaway' together with servicing instructions for the 'Duomatic' hub.
D) See Chapter 3 – Additional Reading). This includes a photograph of Alex Moulton with the prototype 'Stowaway' referred to in Note 3) above.
E) See Chapter 6 – Additional Reading C) for Colin Martin's 'Marathon' ride.
F) See Chapter 3 – Additional Reading). This includes a photograph of Alex Moulton with a mid–1970's prototype 12 speed bicycle incorporating a 'Stowaway' main beam joint. (CF. Note 1) above).

CHAPTER 8

VARIATIONS

One of the most remarkable facts about the Moulton bicycle is the wide range of different versions which were produced. All employed the same basic design philosophy yet the markets catered for included utility, touring, racing and 'car boot' cyclists.

At one time Post Office and 'Minivan' delivery prototypes were mooted. British Rail even experimented with a Moulton fitted with a third wheel on an outrigger which was designed to be ridden along railway lines as a track inspection trolley.

Alex Moulton was granted U.S. and British Patents for a moped based on his bicycle design but this was never commercially produced[1]. There was also a Moulton 'Pedalo' boat which was entered in a competition organised by a glass fibre manufacturer. And in Bristol you can buy hot dogs from a 'Speedsix' fitted with a vending side-car!

This Chapter sets out to log the various marketed versions of the Moulton together with some of the prototypes which never reached the production stage. As the 'Standard' was the original base model its specification is given in greater detail than the other versions.

The definition of a 'Series Two' Moulton can be rather nebulous. The complete 'Series Two' design involved the use of the stronger straight pressed rear forks, pressed front forks and an edge-brazed frame including the detail changes referred to in Chapter 4 such as the plug-in rear carrier and brazed-on carrier strut and tie. Such machines, however, did not arrive on the market in any numbers until some time after Raleigh took control of Moulton Bicycles Limited; rather, the individual assemblies were introduced one at a time.

Initially in 1965, the 'Series Two' rear forks came into use. Later, the re-designed frame began to appear, although it was not illustrated in the main catalogue until 1967. Last came the pressed front forks which were introduced by Raleigh. (Their early 'Procreation' catalogue clearly shows the

'Series One' forks with brazed-in drop-outs). Consequently it could be argued that the late Raleigh machines were the only true mass produced 'Series Twos'.

My feeling is that this would be too purist an attitude and, because in the past the terms 'New Look' and 'Series Two' have been used synonymously, I have consulted the original 'New Look' sales literature and used this as the basis for drawing an arbitrary line between 'Series One' and 'Series Two' machines. Consequently I have described any bicycle which had factory-fitted pressed rear forks as a 'Series Two' Moulton. Where it is important to distinguish between wholly or partly 'Series Two' machines this has been done in the text.

Page from the 1965 Moulton catalogue when the widest range of models was offered.

It should be noted that Moulton specification changes did not necessarily occur 'at a stroke' and consequently some hybrid machines may be encountered. Other deviations from published specifications may have been caused by the prevailing component supply situation. Moultons produced by Raleigh tended to contain a higher proportion of 'in-house' components as time passed. For example, Brooks saddles replaced Middlemores and Raleigh pedals were substituted for those by Union or Phillips.

Catalogue Numbers shown are those used prior to the Raleigh takeover.

16" and 17" Wheel Models.

'Standard' M1

Frame: Nominally 19¾", designed to cover the range of conventional frame sizes from 19¾" to 25". (Maximum effective seat tube length was 27"). Designed to cater for riders from 10 or 11 years of age to 6' 3" tall.

Main Beam – 28¾" x 2½" x 1½". **Seat Tube** – 19¾" from centre of bottom bracket axle to top of tube, cross-section 1 3/8" x 1¾" below junction with cross-bar, tapering to 1 1/8" x 1 1/8" above. **Cross-bar** – cross-section 1¼" x 15/16", was 12¼" in length from junction with main beam to junction with seat tube and then extended 23" behind seat tube to support rear carrier, tapering to ¾" diameter. (True 'Series Two' frames had a plug-in rear carrier). **Head Tube** – 13 5/8" long, tapering from 1½" at base to 1¼". Head and seat tubes parallel – 69° for 'Series One' (except very first machines which were non-parallel) and 70° for 'Series Two'. (Later Raleigh-built machines appear to have had 72° seat tube). **Wheelbase** – 44½". **Bottom Bracket Height** – 'Series One' 11½" unladen, 10½" laden; 'Series Two' 12" unladen, 11" laden. **Cable Guides** – originally brazed-on; from 1965 plastic 'push-in' type.

Forks: Front – round tapered blades (¾" to ½"). 1" rake, solid forged drop-outs. (True 'Series Two' front forks were 'pressed and finned' but did not appear on the 'Standard').

Rear – 'Series One', separate blades 14¾" overall tapered from 1" at rear of top plate to 5/8" at drop-out, connected by pivot to main beam, solid forged forward drop-outs. Originally the blades were linked by a folded top plate. Later an additional plate was brazed to the underside and the design of this plate varied slightly until the 'Series Two' rear fork was introduced in 1965.

– 'Series Two', a much stronger unit using substantially straight forks of 'pressed and finned' construction, the forward drop-outs being of laminated pressed steel. Fitting these forks results in the rear of the machine sitting higher off the ground thus giving steeper angles and a higher bottom bracket. A rim dynamo bracket was brazed to the left hand fork blade.

Wheels: Type E3J Dunlop 'Endrick' pattern rims in chromed steel with dimpled spoke holes (36 hole until 1964, thereafter 28 hole). Phillips small-flange chromed steel front hub. Sturmey-Archer rear hub (see 'Gears' below). Torrington rustless spokes.

Tyres: Dunlop special 16" x 1 3/8" (37 – 349) ribbed black utility tyre based on the Sprite design. Originally these tyres had cotton fabric but this was later changed to nylon which greatly improved durability and helped further reduce rolling resistance. Nylon corded tyres are marked accordingly on the side walls. Dunlop ceased production of bicycle tyres in 1972 whereafter a very similar tyre was made for Raleigh in Poland and sold as the 'Raleigh S.W. Nylon'. (See 'Tyre' section in Appendix).

The original recommended tyre pressure for the Dunlop tyre was 50 pounds per square inch, later modified to '50–60' p.s.i. The Raleigh tyre was designed to run at 55 p.s.i.

Handlebars: Phillips 20" chromed steel all-rounder type on steel stem with 2¾" forward extension giving 4" maximum adjustment (with a minimum of 2½" of stem in the head tube). Lamp bracket on forward extension. Plastic handgrips. T.D. Cross head fittings.

Brakes: Phillips chromed steel calipers with hooded levers. (Minimum and maximum distances from centre line of brake block bolts to centre line of caliper pivot are 2¼" and 3" respectively). With 'Series Two' machines it was necessary to use a front caliper brake at the rear because the short pivot bolt of a conventional rear brake was not long enough to pass right through the 'Series Two' rear fork.

Chainset: Nicklin 52 tooth chainwheel with 6½" cranks in chromed steel. T.D.C. bottom bracket set (English thread) with No. 5 axle. White polythene clip-on chainring cover.

Pedals: 'Series One', Phillips rubber type. 'Series Two', Union rubber reflector type. (Both types fitted with ball bearings).

Gear: 'Series One', Sturmey-Archer A.W. three-speed wide ratio giving 45 – 60 – 80" with 14 tooth sprocket. 'Series Two', Sturmey-Archer F.W. four-speed giving 43 – 51 – 64 – 81" with 13 tooth sprocket. In both cases a handlebar trigger changer was used. From about 1965 a special 50 thou inner gear change cable was fitted to resist stretching which, with the long cable, could lead to misadjustment and slipping of the gears.

(NB: In Britain bicycle gears are traditionally expressed in inches to represent the diameter of the equivalent directly driven front wheel of an 'Ordinary' or 'Penny Farthing'. Hence the number of teeth on the rear sprocket is divided into the number on the chainwheel and multiplied by the wheel diameter in inches[2]).

Saddle: Middlemores special mattress type with no main springs. (The usual large coil springs would have resulted in less efficient pedalling and in any case were not required for comfort because of the suspension system). The 12" x 1" steel seat pillar gave a maximum of 7¼" adjustment, with a minimum of 3" of pillar remaining in the seat tube.

Mudguards: 2" wide deep domed section in steel with non-rust stays bolted to threaded eyes incorporated in the fork ends. Originally only one pair of rear stays were fitted which resulted in the rear guard working loose. A second pair of rear stays was soon incorporated as standard. A front mudflap was sometimes fitted which was a useful accessory as it prevented a lot of mud from being thrown onto the underside of the main beam and around the bottom bracket.

Suspension: Set for weight distribution of 65% over rear axle and 35% over front wheel. **Front:** Coaxial rubber column and steel coil spring (with steel rebound spring) acting in axial compression in single telescopic column in head tube, using steel splines moving in a nylon bush for directional control. **Rear:** Progressive rate trailing rear forks using rubber in shear and compression.

Carrier: Integral rear carrier of ¼" steel tubing with reinforcing gussets, designed to carry 50 lbs. of luggage, with screwed and bolted-on strut and tie. (True 'Series Two' frames had a plug-in carrier and brazed-on strut and tie). Frame had brazed-on fittings to take optional frame-fixed front carrier to accommodate an additional 20 lbs. of luggage. The front bolt fixing on frames built up to early 1964 is higher up the head tube than that found on later frames because of a redesign of the carrier back-guard. (Early Moulton front carriers had a triangular back-guard, later ones a flat topped type to match the rear carrier).

Finish: Originally polychromatic blue or flamboyant red enamel. The latter option was soon changed to pale grey.

Pump: Early machines had a full length pump, the rear peg being brazed to the carrier and the front peg being a bolted-on 'Cyclo' type. Later a short pump was fitted entirely under the carrier to which both pegs were brazed.

Weight: 'Series One', 33 lbs. 'Series Two, 34¾ lbs.

Price: 'Series One', at launch £26 9s. 6d. (£26.48), later £27 19s. 6d. (£27.98). 'Series Two', at launch £29 gns. (£30.45).

Production Dates: The 'Standard' was announced at the Cycle Show in November 1962. Production began at Bradford-on-Avon in March 1963 and later that year was transferred to the B.M.C. plant at Kirkby near Liverpool. The 'Series Two' or 'New Look' Standard was introduced in 1965. The 'Standard' was discontinued in 1966 but re-emerged as the 'Major' after the Raleigh take-over in 1967. It was finally phased out in 1970 when all 'Series Two' production ceased. In effect it was replaced by the 'Mk III'.

'Demonstrator'

This appears to have been a dealers' demonstration model based on the 'Standard' and finished in white.

'Major'

This was really a re-launched 'Standard' and was introduced into the range by Raleigh shortly after they acquired Moulton Bicycles Limited. In almost all respects it was similar to the 'Series Two' 'Standard' but it featured the constructional detail changes described in Chapter 4. The head tube angle was 70° whereas that of the seat tube was 72°.

A 'Brooks' mattress saddle with rear coil springs was fitted in place of the original 'Middlemores' saddle. The 'Major' also had an "Oglaend' type drop stand fitted to the underside of the rear forks. The frame was finished in flamenco red, electric blue or bronze green.

Production of Sturmey-Archer F.W. four speed gears ceased in 1968 and it is probable that late examples of the 'Major' were fitted with A.W. three-speeds.

'Continental' MO
Two models had the catalogue number 'MO' Originally this signified the Moulton 'Continental', the cheapest model in the range, which was announced in 1964. The specification was similar to that of the 'Standard' except that a 'Continental Style' Perry Coaster B500 back-pedal brake was fitted. This gave a fixed gear of 60" with the standard 14 tooth sprocket.

The 'Continenal' was available in polychromatic blue or pale grey. Originally it sold for £24 19s. 6d. (£24.98) which later rose to 26 gns. (£27.30). It was replaced by the 'Automatic' in 1965.

'Automatic' MO
The 'Automatic' was finished in polychromatic holly green or ruby red and differed from the 'Standard' in that it incorporated a prop stand, front fork lock and the 'Duomatic' two-speed back-pedal brake by Fichtel and Sachs.

The prop stand was the original Moulton chromed steel type which was available as an optional extra for other models in the range. It clamped to the carrier beam immediately behind the seat tube and folded away under the carrier. Consequently, it was a very long affair and not particularly robust.

The fork lock was of the Continental 'slide bolt' type and Moultons were probably the first cycle makers to market the device in Britain. The lock casing was brazed to the front fork and when the bicycle was parked the slide bolt was pushed into the locked position thus fouling the spokes and demobilising the machine. This action also released the key which was otherwise held in the lock. (These locks were also fitted to 'S' range Moultons).

Somewhat stangely, it seems that some 'Automatics' were built with 'Series One' rear forks and a true 'Series Two' frame (i.e. edge-brazed with plug-in rear carrier).

The two speed back-pedal brake fitted to the 'Automatic' was of German manufacture and the gear was changed by turning the pedals back by a quarter revolution. Braking was effected by a half back turn of the pedals. Consequently any halt made whilst riding in top gear ensured that the bicycle was automatically in low gear for the restart. This gear also obviated the need for rear brake and gear cables. (See Chapter 7 and the 'Gears' section of the Appendix for further details).

In its standard form the 29 gns (£30.45) 'Automatic' gave a low gear of 46" and a 63" top gear (with 18 tooth sprocket). For 2s. (10p) the rear sprocket could be changed to give, say, in flat terrain gears of 64" and 87" (13 T), or in hilly country 42" and 57" gears (20 T).

The 'Automatic' was withdrawn in 1966.

'Deluxe' M2

The 'Deluxe' and the 'Standard' were the biggest selling 16" wheeled versions of the Moulton. The 'Deluxe' also had the longest production run, commencing in 1963 and ending (as the 'Major Deluxe') in 1970. The main differences from the 'Standard' specification were as follows:

Early 'Series One'. The frame was finished in flamboyant kingfisher blue or flamboyant red with white seat and head tube peaks. The tyres were amber-wall 16 x 1 3/8" Dunlop Sprites, designed to run at 70 p.s.i. 21" wide G.B. alloy all-rounder handlebars were fitted on a G.B. alloy 2½" forward extension. The lamp bracket was fitted to the top headset fittings.

The brakes were G.B. Sprite T91 side-pulls with 126s alloy levers. A front carrier was fitted as standard. The 'Deluxe' had a special 'Middlemores' saddle without main springs but with a better padded top than the 'Standard' saddle. The 'Deluxe' saddle frame was of chromed wire rather than steel strip. (Later the 'Deluxe' saddle was also fitted to the 'Standard' and 'Stowaway'. The Prototype 'Deluxe' was equipped with a Brooks B22 mattress saddle).

The pedals were Phillips reflector type and a rear holdall by Arrowsmith was supplied. The pump was a 15" Britannialloy type and 'special' handlebar grips were fitted. The four speed hub originally offered 40 – 47 – 60 and 76" gears via a 14 tooth sprocket but this was soon changed to 43 – 51 – 64 and 81" by fitting a 13 tooth sprocket.

This version of the 'Deluxe' weighed 34½ lb. fully equipped and cost £31 19s 6d. (£31.98).

Later 'Series One'. The frame was finished in polychromatic holly green or polychromatic midnight blue with chrome mudguards. Steel components, as used on the 'Standard' were substituted for the alloy parts and 'Standard' type black tyres were fitted.

A chromed steel secondary chain-guard of more conventional design was also fitted to supplement the white polythene chainwheel guard which, on its own, was insufficient to prevent all risk of torn or oily trousers (personal experience!).

The price was 33 gns (£34.65).

'Series Two'. The finishes were as for later 'Series One' 'Deluxes' but the front carrier and steel chain-guard were dispensed with. An Oglaend prop stand was fitted to the underside of the redesigned rear forks, clear of the pedals. This was a great improvement on the original Moulton prop stand (see the 'Automatic' above) but could not be fitted to existing machines unless the whole rear fork assembly was replaced, the fixing being brazed on.

For the first time integral lighting was offered as standard (to compete with the Raleigh RSW16). This involved a Miller rim driven dynamo fitted to the brazed-on bracket on the rear forks. From 1967 a factory-fitted GH6 Dynohub could be included in the specification at extra cost.

The 'New Look' M2 weighed 38½ lbs. in standard form and cost 33 gns. (£34.65) when launched in 1965. By May 1967 the price was £35 3s 4d. (£35.17) or £37 5s 11d. (£37.30) with Dynohub lighting.

'Major Deluxe'.

This was the Raleigh version of the 'Deluxe' and was offered in flamenco red, electric blue or bronze green. The specification was all as for the 'Major' but also included a Sturmey-Archer GH6 Dynohub lighting set and a holdall as standard.

'S Deluxe' MS2.

In common with the other 'S' range models this was handbuilt at Bradford-on-Avon. It was similar to the M2 'Deluxe' but featured Dunlop 17 x 1¼" high pressure tyres on alloy rims and G.B. alloy handlebars, stem and Coureur brakes. The mudguards were Bluemels Club Specials (lightweight plastic).

An alloy seat pillar was fitted complete with special mattress saddle. The front hub was a B.H. (British Hub Company) Airlite. A spoke lock was fitted to the front forks. (See the 'Automatic' above). The chainset was a Williams

AB77 alloy cotterless type with 6¾" cranks and a 54 tooth chainring over which the steel 'Deluxe' type chain cover was fitted. All cables were concealed in the frame. Like the other 'S' models, the 'S Deluxe' was available with a fully chromed frame if required.

The basic price, when launched in 1965, was £49 19s. 6d. (£49.98).

'Safari' M3 and MS3

The Moulton 'Safari' and its 'S' range variant are described in Chapter 6.

'Speed' M4

The original M4 'Speed' racing model is described in Chapter 5. That model, however, was never actually marketed and the commercially available 'Speed' was basically a 'Standard' with a racier riding position. It was fitted with down-turned all-rounder handlebars on a 3½" steel stem, steel pedals and a Middlemores leather sports saddle (some were perforated, others cutaway).

A short alloy pump was supplied. The frame finish was colorado red with chrome mudguards and a special black holdall was supplied.

When introduced in 1964 the 'Speed' M4 cost £29 19s. 6d. which rose to 31 gns (£32.55). The 'Speed' was withdrawn in 1966.

'Stowaway' M5 and MS5

These models are described in Chapter 7.

'Speedsix' M6

The 'Speedsix' is described in Chapter 5. It is worth noting that extra wide 'Series Two' rear forks were fitted to this machine in order to accommodate the derailleur block.

'S' Speed

This model is described in Chapter 5.

Moulton 'Mk III'

The 'Mk III' was developed by Alex Moulton in conjunction with Raleigh. It was launched by the Nottingham Company, together with the 'Chopper' and 'RSW Mk III' in 1970. The Moulton 'Mk III' was available in white, tropic blue or royal carmine, in each case the trim being in satin black.

The frame, ahead of the seat tube, was basically similar to the previous Moultons although the jointing of the main beam to the head tube, and the tapering of the head and seat tubes was slightly different. The control cables were run under the main beam in wide steel loops. Steel all-rounder handlebars and a Raleigh S525 mattress saddle[3] were fitted. No integral lighting system was provided.

The original chainwheel design was retained but manufactured by Raleigh rather than Nicklin. The circular plastic chainwheel guard was constructed of a more rigid material than hitherto (which kept its shape better) and was finished in black with a red inner ring. It was behind the seat tube, however, that the 'Mk III' differed most from its predecessors.

Instead of the trailing arm pattern of rear fork suspension adopted on previous Moultons, the 'Mk III' featured a triangulated rear fork assembly. One end of the triangle base pivoted immediately behind the bottom bracket, in theory a better pivot point than that previously used. The other end of the triangle base was formed by the rear wheel axle drop-outs. The apex of the triangle bore onto a rubber 'squashball' which formed the suspension medium and which was mounted against the back of the seat tube near its junction with the cross-bar. Consequently a very strong rear suspension resulted, although the ride was firmer than that offered by 'Series One and Two' machines.

The rear carrier was also different. Instead of the cross-bar passing through the seat tube and thus forming a fixed carrier beam, there was a completely detachable carrier bolted to the plate on the back of the seat tube to which the 'squashball' was attached. The carrier was braced up by a thin strut running from near the central underside of the carrier to a position a few inches above the bottom bracket. Under the carrier was a full length Clarion pump, a welcome feature after the juvenile inflators fitted to most earlier mass produced Moultons. A slightly remodelled holdall was available as an extra but, sadly, there was no provision for a front carrier.

Other features included integral prop stand, this time fitted under the bottom bracket. The seat tube height was slightly reduced to give a basic frame size of 18½", thus making the bike more suitable for 8 – 9 year olds. The newly launched Sturmey-Archer S3B hub was fitted, this being a three speed gear based on the A.W. and incorporating a new, compact, cable-operated hub brake. A 13 tooth sprocket was supplied, giving 48, 64 and 85" gears. The 'Mk III' was therefore the highest geared mass produced utility version of the Moulton.

The wheelbase was reduced by 3½" to 41" thus changing the Moulton from a very long wheelbase bicycle to one with a more 'normal' wheelbase. The bottom bracket height was also reduced slightly to 10½" under load. A Raleigh-threaded wide bottom bracket was provided which precludes the easy fitting of most good quality cotterless chainsets. (Usually the 'Mk III' bottom bracket must be cut down and rethreaded for this purpose). The 'Mk III' was designed to have 70½° parallel head and seat tubes but production machines appear to have had 71° seat and 70° head tubes.

Although the 'Mk III' was offered in only one version, it was relatively easy to re-equip to suit most cyclists' needs. Like most Raleigh products it was well finished and strongly constructed, although some cost cutting practices were indulged in. For instance, the front forks were cheap pressed units[4]. However, some interesting 'Mk III' conversions exist incorporating lightweight fittings, 1¼" high pressure tyres, increased gearing options and forks rebuilt in Reynolds 531 lightweight tubing.

The standard 'Mk III' weighed 35 lbs. and cost £37 when introduced in 1970. Sales did not meet Raleigh's expectations and production ceased in 1974.

Export Models

At one time the Moulton bicycle was sold in about 30 countries world-wide. In most cases the bikes were exported from England, usually in C.K.D. (Completely Knocked Down) form but some licensed production was also undertaken. Usually the models sold abroad were based on the 'Standard' or 'Stowaway'. The 'S' range models were also exported. (From Bradford-on-Avon).

The following are some of the firms which marketed the Moulton overseas:

Denmark: Nellemann & Drewsen A/S (Copenhagen).

Sweden: Fram-King Import AB (Halsingborg).

Norway: Jonas Oglaend (DBS) (Oslo). This firm, which made the Moulton 'Series Two' prop stand, produced a special 'Stowaway' for the Norwegian market. To suit cobbled and snow covered streets it was equipped with massive 1 5/8" Dunlop tyres which looked almost as horrific as the 2" ones used on the original 'RSW16'.

The front wheel had a drum brake and the rear wheel was fitted with a single speed back-pedal brake. The frame was basically 'Series Two' and a U.S. style one-piece crank set was fitted, complete with metal pedals and toe-clips. The 'DBS Stowaway' also had the chromed steel 'Deluxe' type chainguard.

Netherlands: Stokvis International (Rotterdam) marketed the Moulton in fixed frame and 'Stowaway' forms in the Netherlands using the advertising slogan 'De fiets van deze tijd' which, roughly translated, means, 'The bike of this time'. The Moulton even appeared on a Stokvis calendar.

Belgium and Luxembourg: Stokvis International (Brussels) sold the 'Stowaway' in this market emphasising its usefulness as a 'car boot' commuter's bicycle.

West Germany: F. Lichtenfels K.G. (Dusseldorf) sold the 'Stowaway' XM5 and 'Continental' XM0.

Switzerland: 'Allegro' – Arnold Grandjean S.A. (Marin-Neuchatel) were the Swiss agents for Moulton bicycles.

Canada: C.C.M. (Canadian Cycle & Motor) marketed the Moulton '4 Speed' in Canada. This model is briefly described in Chapter 6, being the bicycle which Tim Woodman rode across Canada. Canadian '4 Speeds' were fitted with plug-in rear carriers before this became a standard feature on domestic models.

U.S.A.: Huffman Manufacturing Company (Dayton, Ohio and Azusa, California) produced about 5000 Moultons from C.K.D. kits between October 1963 and Autumn 1966, and, at one time, intended to manufacture complete machines. Indeed a production prototype was submitted to Alex Moulton for approval.

The 'Huffy Moulton 4 Speed' (Model 2101) had twin carriers, prop stand, toolset and white wall Dunlop 'Sprite' tyres but was otherwise similar to the 'Standard'. Later versions were called the 'Mk III' (not to be confused with the Raleigh built 'Mk III'). and featured a rigid plastic wrap-round chainguard in addition to the usual Moulton polythene chainwheel guard. Bags and baskets were optional extras.

'Huffy' also produced a 'Stateside' version of the 'Stowaway' which had a prop stand, white wall tyres, 60" gear and twin carriers (Chevrolet trunks being larger than Austin 1100 boots!).

A very small number of 'Safaris' were imported by Huffmann. Most of the Moultons marketed by this company were distributed on the west coast of the U.S.A. although a few were sold in New York City.

Raleigh Industries of America, Incorporated, imported Moultons twice in late 1971. Approximately 1,000 bicycles were involved but the company discontinued imports because of 'lack of consumer interest'. This was hardly surprising as Raleigh admit that they 'never prepared any promotional literature for the Moulton'.

South Africa: Raleigh (South Africa) manufactured the Moulton under licence during the very period when their parent company was locked in a trade war with Moulton Bicycles Limited in the U.K. (See Note 1) to Chapter 4).

Prototypes

A considerable number of designs were produced at Bradford-on-Avon which, for various reasons, never went into production. These fall into four main categories;

1). Evolutionary Prototypes for the 'Series One' Moulton
The most important of these are described in Chapter 2.

2). Prototypes Produced Between 1963 and the 1967 Raleigh Takeover
These include the **M9 'Stowaway'** (see Chapter 7) and the Moulton **'Carrier'**. The latter was announced at the Brighton Show in September 1965 and had a huge pair of wicker baskets mounted fore and aft in special reinforced carriers with additional bracing struts and ties. A large double prop stand was fitted to the front carrier. The tyres were 16 x 1¾".

The Moulton **'Bastard'** was a sort of hybrid Moulton/RSW16 with balloon tyres but this appears to have been more of a joke than a serious prototype.

3). Prototypes Produced for Raleigh After the Take-over
Quite a number of these were made, many of which were part of the 'Mk III' evolutionary programme. The **'Marathon'**, ridden to Australia by Colin Martin was actually a modified pre-production 'Mk III' prototype (see Chapter 6).

The **'Fun'** was basically a 'Mk III' without a rear carrier and fitted with plastic mudguards, a Sturmey-Archer five-speed hub gear and very short alloy all-rounder handlebars (on an adjustable reach stem) with very long brake levers.

Several prototypes without front suspension were made at Raleigh's instigation, the most interesting of which was the Moulton **'Twenty'** which was similar to a 'Mk III' but with '20' wheels. Hence, it looked reminiscent of a Raleigh '20' with rear suspension.

4). Prototypes Produced After Raleigh Ceased Production of the Moulton
These are mainly advanced lightweight machines including further developments of the 'Mk III'. Many incorporate the Moulton 'Stowaway' main beam joint and special 'Swan Neck' handlebar stems. These prototypes form the early part of the evolutionary process leading to the launch of the new 'Alex Moulton' bicycles in 1983.

14" Wheel Models

Triang 'Junior 1970'
This was the first 14" wheel version of the Moulton and was a juvenile machine made under licence by Lines Brothers, the toy manufacturers. It was designed to cater for the 6 – 10 year olds. The 'Junior 1970' incorporated working rear suspension and a semi-sprung front end. (The rubber bellows were toughened up to act as the springing medium. The handlebars were not sprung but the front end of the frame was).

14 x 1 3/8" pneumatic tyres, a frame-fixed circular plastic chainguard and twin caliper brakes were included in the specification. The saddle was a two-tone mattress type and a plastic pump was supplied.

The 'Junior 1970' cost 16 gns. (£16.80) when launched in 1965.

The 'Mini' Range

The original Moulton frame was designed around the average British male adult whereas the 'Mini', in common with the 'RSW16', was based on the average female. Thus the 'Mini' was able to cater for riders from 6 years of age to adults of 5' 8", depending on the fittings with which is was equipped.

In most respects the 'Mini' was a 7/8th scale version of the original Moulton design and, broadly speaking, this applied even to weight and price. The wheels were 14 x 1 3/8" with E2J rims in steel, except for the 'Mini Automatic' which had alloy rims. The frame used parallel sided round section tubing for all but the main beam. Edge brazed joints were employed and the rear carrier together with its stays were brazed on. It was originally intended that a front carrier should be offered as an optional extra and some machines were built with brazed-on fixing points. The Raleigh take-over seems to have put an end to this proposal.

The front suspension was a scaled down version of the original unit but the rear forks used an unbonded rubber wedge in compression only (as opposed to the progressive rate compression and shear system used on 'Series One and Two' machines). The fork ends were pressed rather than brazed in and the rear forks had rear entry ends. Some versions had a brazed-on dynamo bracket on the left hand rear fork blade. A brazed-on prop stand was fitted to the underside of the rear forks on some models.

The head and seat tube angles were 70° and the nominal frame size was 15". Front fork rake was 7/8" and the bottom bracket height was 11" unladen, 9 15/16" laden. The wheelbase, at 39", was 5½" shorter than the 16" wheel Moulton.

The quick-release seat pillar was wider than that used on the senior models, being 1 1/8" diameter and, on those models with adult fittings, 13" long. This gave a maximum effective seat tube length of 23" (with 3" of seat pillar remaining in the tube). Narrow (17") steel all-rounder handlebars were fitted. The handlebar stem was of standard diameter and, in models with adult fittings, gave up to 3" variation in height (with a minimum 2½" of stem in the head tube). The stem was originally intended to be a quick-release type but there seems to have been an ambivalent attitude to this point. Many machines were made with quick-release stems and clamps but with a plain nut instead of a quick-release lever. Others were fitted with conventional cone type stems.

The chainwheel was the familiar Nicklin type with polythene guard as used on the full-size models.

The 'Mini' range was commercially very successful being in production in various forms from 1966 to 1974. Many of the later Raleigh-made models had no front suspension (contrary to Dr. Moulton's advice). This resulted in overstressing of the head tube/main beam junction leading to fracturing of the frame. This in turn necessitated recalls (as late as 1977) and the production of a 'free issue' two part clamp to reinforce the affected joint.

The models which comprised the 'Mini' range were as follows:

'Mini' M7

The 'Mini', introduced early in 1966, was equipped with 5½" cranks and narrow pedals. The seat pillar gave up to 7" adjustment and the machine was originally intended for children of 7 years upwards to adults of 5' 6". (Although Raleigh later advertised it for 6 year olds). The handlebar stem had a 1" forward extension and Dunlop block tread utility tyres were fitted.

A 58" single speed back-pedal brake was fitted and the bike was available in cherry red or caribbean blue. It weighed 31 lb. and sold for 19 gns (£19.95) when first marketed.

By 1967 the back-pedal brake had been replaced by a cable operated caliper brake. After Raleigh acquired Moulton Bicycles Limited the choice of frame colours became royal carmine, caribbean blue (later deleted) or sunset yellow. Raleigh later produced the 'Mini' without front suspension[5] but the original fully sprung machine continued in production for a while as the **'Mini Deluxe'**. This had a prop stand, wider handlebars and 20 spoke wheels.

'Mini Automatic' M8

This model, launched in the summer of 1966, was in direct competition with the similarly priced but much heavier 'RSW 16'. (The 'RSW' weighed about 44 lb., the 'Mini Automatic' about 36 lb.). The 'Mini Automatic' had 6½" cranks with full size pedals plus Miller dynamo lighting, Arrowsmith holdall, prop stand and the Fichtel & Sachs 'Torpedo-Duomatic' two speed back-pedal brake.

The saddle was a special 'Middlemores' mattress type (without main coil springs). The 14" x 1 3/8" tyres were a smaller version of the special Dunlop ribbed type used on larger Moultons and were fitted to alloy rims. The M8 was finished in Autumn gold.

The 'Mini Automatic' cost 29½ gns. (£30.98) when launched. It was discontinued in 1967.

'Super 4' M1

When, in 1967, the 'Standard' was discontinued it was effectively replaced by the 'Super 4' which, like the 'Mini Automatic' was one of the best interpretations of the Moulton Mini range.

The 'Super 4' came equipped with 6½" cranks and reflector pedals. It could be ridden by 8 year olds or adults up to 5' 8" tall. The bike was originally catalogued with a 2¾" forward handlebar extension but most had a 1" extension. The saddle and tyres were as the M8 above but twin caliper brakes were fitted and variable gearing was achieved by use of a Sturmey-Archer F.W. four speed hub giving gears of 38 – 44 – 56 and 71".

When announced in 1967 the 'Super 4' cost £25 4s. 0d. (£25.20). It weighed about 34 lbs.

The 'Super 4' was originally offered in cherry red or caribbean blue. Raleigh continued production of the machine in royal carmine, flamboyant green or caribbean blue. They also fitted a Brooks mattress saddle **with** main coil springs.

The F.W. four-speed was discontinued in 1968 and hence, in 1969, an A.W. three-speed version of the 'Super 4' emerged. This was known as the **'Minx'**. Subsequently the front suspension was dispensed with and the result was the **'Midi'** which, like the 'Minis' with unsprung front forks[5], was subject to cracking of the frame at the head tube/main beam junction. The 'Midi' was available in 'pop' purple, sky blue or flamboyant green. Conventional block treaded tyres were fitted.

'Stowaway' M9

This model, which never went into commercial production is described in Chapter 7.

Accessories

A number of special accessories were made for the Moulton. These included front and rear holdalls, for the 'Standard', 'Deluxe', 'Speed' and 'Safari' at

1964 prices ranging from £1 18s. 5d. (£1.93) to £3 4s. 8d. (£3.23). A 'Mini' holdall cost £2 0s. 6d. (£2.03) in 1967. Most of these bags were made by Arrowsmith. Rear holdalls were also made for the 'Mk III'.

Front and rear willow baskets, designed to fit on the integral carriers, were also available and in 1967 these cost £1 6s. 9d. (£1.37) and £1 19s. 6d. (£1.98) respectively. A front carrier for full size Moultons cost 19s. 6d. (98p) in 1964. At one time a Moulton bell was available complete with the 'Double M' symbol cast into the centre-piece.

The original long prop stand for senior models cost £1 5s. 0d. (£1.25) in 1964. Dynohub or Miller rim dynamo lighting was usually available at extra cost if required. In 1967 the dynohub added just over £4 to the price whereas the rim dynamo could be fitted for £1 19s 11d. (£2.00). For 'Series One' models (which lacked a brazed-on dynamo bracket) a specially reinforced rear mudguard stay was available onto which the rim dynamo could be fixed. Dunlop tyre pressure gauges were available at 9s 4d. (47p).

A rare but interesting Moulton accessory, introduced late in 1965, was the child carrier. After much deliberation it was decided that the best solution to the problem of carrying an infant passenger was for the child to sit on its own saddle ahead of the rider and between his or her arms. Hence a small saddle with back and foot rests was produced and this was mounted on a simple frame which clamped to the main beam and head tube. This item cost £2 9s. 11d. (£2.50) in 1967 but very few were produced.

The advent of the Moulton also led to the introduction of cyclometers for 16" wheels by makers such as Lucas and Huret.

Notes

1) The relevant patent numbers for the Moulton Moped are:
   a) British Patent No. 1074 431. Filed 17th March 1965, granted 5th July 1967.
   b) U.S. Patent No. 3,280,932. Filed 18th March 1965.

   The patents cover the use of a rear wheel under 20" diameter with a hub gear incorporating two freewheels, one driven by a conventional pedal-operated chainwheel, the other by a motor.
   (N.B. Raleigh produced a moped version of the 'RSW 16'. This was called the 'Wisp' and utilised conventional moped transmission).
2) This does *not* give the distance which the machine will travel along the ground for one revolution of the pedals, as incorrectly stated in the June 1981 edition of Ron Kitching's 'Everything Cycling' catalogue. To obtain that distance it is necessary to multiply the gear in inches by π < (Pi). The resulting figure is known as the 'development' and is widely used on the continent where it is expressed in metres.
   Strictly speaking a gear expressed in inches is not a ratio but the term is so commonly used in this context that it has also been adopted from time to time in this book.
3) This saddle was similar to the original Middlemores type fitted to the 'Standard'.
4) Two types of pressed front fork were fitted to the 'Mk III', one being the 'finned' type used on late Raleigh-built 'Series Two' Moultons. The other type were simply tapered down to the drop-out in the conventional manner.
5) 'Midis' and later unsprung 'Minis' featured a head tube which tapered down towards the top and bottom in place of the original parallel sided tube.

Additional Reading – Primary Sources

A) Catalogues produced by Moulton Bicycles Limited and Raleigh Industries Limited between 1963 and 1972.

B) See Chapter 3, Additional Reading A). This gives a detailed specification of a prototype 'Series One' 'Deluxe' but many of the dimensions given differ from the production model. (Illustrated).

C) See Chapter 3, Additional Reading M). This gives much useful information about the introduction of the 'Mini' range (Illustrated).

D) 'Moulton Last-Minute Lines' Motor Cycle and Cycle Trader, 17th September 1965, p.257. News item on the introduction of the child seat and carrier bicycle. (Illustrated).

NB: Other references relating to specific models are given in the Additional Reading lists for Chapters 5, 6 and 7.

CHAPTER 9

REAPPRAISAL (TEN YEARS ON)

Since the Moulton was launched late in 1962 many column inches of the cycling press have been devoted to arguments concerning the relative merits of the Moulton bicycle and the classic diamond frame lightweight. Many opinions have been offered, for and against each machine but few protagonists have been in a position to actually scientifically measure the factors involved. Furthermore it is very difficult to obtain relevant hard data.

As mentioned in Chapter 3, 'Design' magazine tested a prototype Moulton 'Deluxe' in 1963. The testers included an E.M.I. Research Psychologist, an Industrial Designer and a representative of the Road Research Laboratory. The Cyclists Touring Club and the Science Museum also acted as advisers. Most of the tests were purely subjective but it was generally agreed that the designer's claims of better roadholding, enhanced acceleration, improved manoeuvrability, greater comfort and superior luggage carrying capacity were well founded. It was also noted that the prototype 'Deluxe' was several pounds lighter than a similarly equipped standard machine.

A number of critical comments were made concerning minor details of the design and most of these were resolved by the time the bicycle went into mass production. The testers also observed that the 'feel' of riding the Moulton is rather different from a conventional machine, especially at low speeds: but as one of the team said, 'The instability at first experienced at low speed became transformed, with more experience, into high manoeuvrability with great precision at both low and high speed'.

Apart from these subjective tests, 'Design' had the suspension tested by E.M.I. Electronics Ltd. at Hayes in Middlesex. The Moulton and a conventional bicycle (presumably a comparable utility version) were ridden by the same person at identical 'moderate' and 'fast' speeds over an obstacle course. The 'bumps' varied from 3 to 6 inches in height and were of different shapes and lengths, some being square edged and others ramped. For instance, one obstacle consisted of a ramp paved with corrugated iron sheeting.

Accelerometers were fixed to the saddle and handlebar stems and the outputs were fed to a Cossor double beam oscilloscope with a camera attachment to film the resulting acceleration wave forms. After analysis of the results, the E.M.I. scientists concluded that 'In general, for the same obstacle, at the same speed, the peak shock levels experienced on the standard bicycle are about twice as great as those on the Moulton bicycle'.

The testers found that, when ridden slowly, the Moulton 'transmitted a more perceptible level of all round vibration' but also that the faster it was ridden and the heavier it was loaded, the more efficient the suspension became.

In August 1964 the Consumers' Association Magazine 'Which?' published a report on the three speed 'Series One' 'Standard' which was tested against a Triumph 'Palm Beach' (a conventional 26" wheel three speed bicycle). The tests indicated that the Moulton would fit a wider range of people than a bicycle of more conventional design and that it was much more comfortable on rough surfaces. Some riders found that they were able to climb hills slightly better with the conventional bicycle. General performance, braking, durability and acceleration were found to be similar for both machines.

'Which?' concluded that for utilitarian purposes and as a machine to be shared by several people (or which could 'grow' with a young person), the Moulton was better value for money than a comparable conventional bicycle. The point was made again that the 'feel' of riding a Moulton was different.

After the publication of these reports many tests of individual Moulton models appeared in the cycling press but these were usually purely subjective. The controversy about the relative effectiveness of the Moulton design continued to flare from time to time; and so, in 1972, some ten years after the launch of his revolutionary bicycle, Alex Moulton decided to carry out directly comparative tests between a Moulton 'Mk III' with lightweight fittings and a conventional classic lightweight. The results were announced by Dr. Moulton in the course of a Friday evening discourse at the Royal Institution, London on 23rd February, 1973.

The two test bicycles each weighed 29 lbs. and rider weight was identical at 180 lbs. The same gear ratios were adopted and the rider position was identical. The Moulton was fitted with Dunlop developed 17 x 1¼" high pressure tyres, whereas the classic bicycle was equipped with 27 x 1¼" high pressure tyres[1]. The pressure adopted for both bicycles' tyres was 70 p.s.i. More than 250 runs were carried out under carefully controlled conditions; over the whole speed range the Moulton was found to have a 6% advantage over the conventional machine.

Further tests were undertaken to isolate in which areas the Moulton's advantage lay. Transmission efficiency was tested, both machines having derailleur gears. No significant difference was found, the efficiency for both machines varying from 96% with the chain running in line, down to 88% with the chain driving the extreme sprocket. The test was then repeated using Sturmey-Archer three speed hubs. Again, no significant difference was found between the two bicycles, the efficiency in direct drive (middle gear) being 97% but dropping to 85% in high and 80% in low gear due to the frictional losses of indirect drive[2]. Wheel bearing variations were also investigated but, perhaps surprisingly, no significant difference in frictional loss was discovered.

However, examination of the power requirements using various tyres proved to be very revealing. It was found that the lowest rolling resistance was achieved with the nylon corded 17 x 1¼" Dunlop tyre at 70 p.s.i.

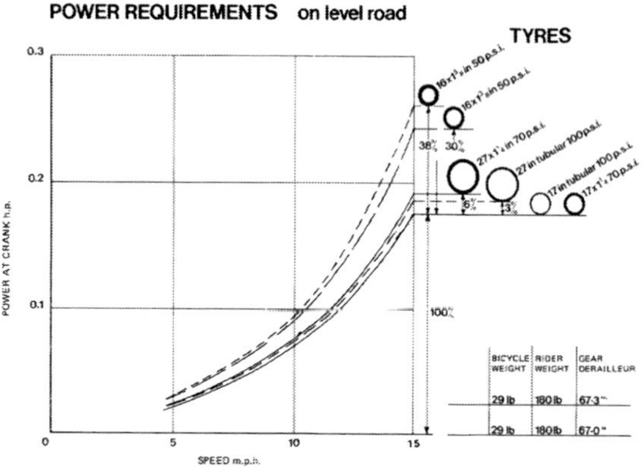

Alex Moulton's table of power requirements for various bicycle tyres, compiled after the 1972 tests.

This actually matched the performance of the equivalent 17" tubular at 100 p.s.i. and required 3½% less power input than a 27" tubular at 100 p.s.i. and 6% less than a 27" x 1¼" high pressure tyre at 70 p.s.i. Tests were also carried out with 16 x 1 3/8" and 16 x 1 5/8" tyres running at 50 p.s.i. and these were 30% and 38% less efficient respectively than the 17" high pressure tyre.

During the course of the tests acceleration was also investigated using electronic timing in an aircraft hanger, and the Moulton demonstrated a 10% advantage over the classic lightweight. In this case the reduced inertia of the small wheels supplements the claimed reduced rolling resistance of the tyres[3].

Anyone who has ridden a Moulton over grass will know that the small-wheeled machine makes heavy going of soft ground when compared with a big-wheeler. This was confirmed by the tests which indicated that the problem was caused by deeper penetration of the tyre into the ground.

The amount of rider energy transmitted to the suspension was investigated and was found to be less than 1% of which not all was actually lost[4]. Consequently it can be seen that the losses thus incurred are minute when compared with, say, using a different tyre or using variable gears. The two machines were also placed on test rigs to analyse the relative smoothness of ride. As one would expect the Moulton came out of this test very well. At 6 Hz (6 'bumps per second' in this context) the Moulton was three times as smooth at the handlebars although for frequencies over 11 Hz the conventional machine was marginally better. However, when it came to saddle comfort the Moulton was superior at all frequencies, being twice as smooth at 4 Hz in terms of R.M.S. 'G' acceleration. After the tests on the rig, the bicycles were fitted with accelerometers to measure smoothness of ride on the road and even on a smooth surface at a leisurely 10 m.p.h., the Moulton was significantly more comfortable.

The effects of added weight on each machine were also investigated and no significant difference resulted, each bicycle showing an increased power requirement of 6% on the flat and 10% on a 1 in 8 hill for a 25 lb. addition in weight.

This research indicates that the Moulton, when fitted with lightweight components and high pressure tyres, is easier to propel, more accelerative and more comfortable than a similarly equipped lightweight of conventional design. The astonishing superiority of the 1¼" tyre over the 1 3/8" type confirms the widely held opinion amongst devotees that the Moulton is at its best on the narrower high pressure tyre.

Not surprisingly the rolling resistance figures for the 1¼" tyre have been hotly debated but it should be noted that no-one seems to have produced directly comparable empirical evidence to contradict Dr. Moulton's claims. F.R. Whitt, the leading British writer on bicycle technology, has given figures for 16 x 1 3/8" utility tyres which show that they compare badly with 27 x 1¼" high pressures but Alex Moulton would not disagree with this. (Moulton's original claim was that the 16 x 1 3/8" tyre, if inflated to around 60 p.s.i., would roll as easily as a 26 x 1 3/8" tyre at the typical lower pressures used by utility riders).

F.R. Whitt has not tested the 17 x 1¼" tyre but considers that it should not roll significantly more easily than the 16 x 1 3/8" as he believes that there is 'no appreciable slowing effect from larger cross-sections as used in bicycle tyre ranges' for a given tyre pressure (see Additional Reading F)). This contradicts the generally held view of most serious cyclists that the narrower and lighter the tyre, the easier it will roll. If Dr. Whitt's theory is true presumably John Woodburn would still have broken the Cardiff–London record on the Moulton if it had been fitted with 16 x 2" RSW balloon tyres, provided that they were inflated to the pressures normally used for tubular racing tyres[5].

So where does this leave the Moulton? In the field of bicycle science, where the power levels are so low and so many variables are involved, subjective opinions must be treated with caution but recently a very well known record breaking cyclist offered the opinion that the lightweight Moulton was just as fast as the conventional racing machine.

My own opinions of how the Moulton compares with the conventional bicycle, assuming similar standards of equipment and tyre widths, are as follows:

a) It is considerably more comfortable under most conditions although on roads with coarse stone chippings there can be considerable low amplitude high frequency handlebar vibration. (This is reflected in Dr. Moulton's findings concerning vibration in excess of 11 Hz. The problem is caused by friction in the suspension system and is likely to have been overcome in the new 'Alex Moulton' bicycle).
b) It is faster over most rough surfaces and roadholding is better under such conditions.

c) It seems to be faster down hills. Some riders find it rather slower on the ascent but there is disagreement on this point. On the level there seems to be little perceptible difference.
d) Wheel damage is less likely to occur but, as one would expect, tyre wear is somewhat more rapid. On the other hand it is easier to carry 16" or 17" spares when on a long tour.
e) Heavy loads can be carried more easily and safely, and in a manner which presents a reduced frontal area for lower wind resistance. The handling of the machine is relatively unaffected by heavy loads and indeed the roadholding seems to improve as the load increases.
f) Initial acceleration (i.e. from a stationery position) is better.
g) The Moulton 17 x 1¼" nylon corded tyre rolls markedly better than the 16 x 1 3/8" tyres including even the nylon corded version of the original Dunlop Sprite-based utility tyre.
h) The Moulton has a different feel to a conventional bicycle, the steering being 'quick' even on long wheelbase versions.

Most people who have ridden a lightweight version of the Moulton, equipped with the 17 x 1¼" tyres, form a favourable opinion of it. Conversely its harshest critics usually have either not ridden a Moulton at all or have compared a utility or juvenile version with a good quality conventional lightweight.

The Moulton has been criticised for being 'oversold' as a multi-role bicycle but the fact remains that, with suitable equipment and modifications, it has been used as a functional utility machine, an excellent tourer, a practical 'car boot' bicycle and a successful racing machine, particularly for pursuit team racing and time trialling.

It is, in my opinion, the only practical design to successfully challenge the pre-eminence of the highly refined conventional diamond frame bicycle; in some respects such as rider comfort, luggage carrying capacity and adjustability, the Moulton clearly surpasses it.

Notes

1) It would be invidious to name the firms involved but the conventional bicycle was made by a very well known English lightweight manufacturer and the tyres, (which had a very similar tread pattern to that used on the Moulton) were made by an internationally renowned maker of French origin.

2) The Royal Institution Discourse transcript quotes 80% efficiency for the hub gear in both high and low modes but Dr. Moulton's test results were actually as quoted here. He considers that the major reason for hub gears being less efficient is that a 'series' loss is involved. i.e. the percentage efficiency of the primary drive (pedals to rear sprocket) is *multiplied* by the percentage efficiency of the final drive (the epicyclic gears in the hub) to give the overall transmission efficiency.

   With derailleur gears there is only a primary drive with *additional* losses introduced by the jockey wheels (very slight) and by the highly flexible chain running out of line.

   This assumes clean, well lubricated gears in both cases. As F.R. Whitt has stated 'a very dirty chain can render the (derailleur) system unworkable with an efficiency of nil'.

   Although most racing cyclists would intuitively agree with Alex Moulton's findings on gears, F.R. Whitt has stated that 'It is probable that there is little to choose between hub and derailleur *on average* for all gears if the same range of gears is assumed for both types i.e.*–33% to +25% of normal'* (See Additional Reading D)).

3) In Additional Reading E), (see below), F.R. Whitt agrees that the smaller wheel should be more accelerative but does not consider the likely improvement to be more than 3%.

4) No doubt a rider with a very clumsy style could lose more power to the suspension and this may explain why some riders in the 1964 'Which?' test found hill climbing slightly easier on a conventional machine.

5) Dr. Whitt considers that at racing speeds the higher rolling resistance of a 16 x 1 3/8" tyre becomes a minimal problem as most of the riders energy is being used to overcome wind resistance.

Additional Reading – Primary Sources

A) Alex Moulton. 'The Moulton Bicycle' Friday Evening Discourse Transcript, Royal Institution, 23rd February 1973. The results of the 1972 tests with many interesting illustrations and graphs.

B) See Chapter 2 Additional Reading E). This includes acceleration wave forms for the suspension tests carried out for 'Design' magazine.

C) 'Moulton Bicycle'. Which? (Consumers Association) 19th August 1964 pp. 246–247. The Moulton 'Standard' is tested here against a Triumph 'Palm Beach' (Illustrated).

Secondary Sources

D) 'Developing Pedal Power' Open University Alternative Technology Group. This is the transcript of a conference held on 14th–15th December 1978, edited by Andrew Brown and Stephen Potter. Among many interesting articles is 'Variable Gears: Some basic Ergonomics and Mechanics' by F.R. Whitt. p.p. 112–141 (Illustrated). This is the most interesting article on bicycle gearing which I have ever encountered. (Incidentally, on p. 131 there is a photograph of a Moulton with rubber-belt drive).

E) See Chapter 2, Additional Reading G). Chapter 6). 'The Wheel and its Rolling Resistance' (p. 121 for acceleration of various wheel formats).

F) F.R. Whitt, M.Sc. 'Tyre and Road Contact' Cycletouring, February/ March 1977, p. 61. In this article Dr. Whitt argues that there is little evidence in favour of narrow section tyres being faster (for a given pressure).

APPENDIX

A) Chronological List of Major Events in the History of the Moulton Bicycle

1957 Alex Moulton investigates optimum riding position.
1958 Development work on the Moulton bicycle begins in earnest.
1959 First patent applied for.
1962 'Safari' tested in Iceland. Moulton bicycle launched at London Cycle and Motor Cycle Show. John Woodburn breaks Cardiff–London record on Moulton 'Speed'.
1963 Production commences at Bradford-on-Avon, later transferred to Kirkby.
1964 Moulton becomes the fashionable utility bicycle. Tim Woodman crosses Canada on Moulton '4 speed'.
1965 Raleigh introduce RSW16. Moulton range at its peak. Vic Nicholson wins 15 major time trials on 'Speedsix'.
1966 'Mini' range launched. Fierce competition from rival manufacturers. Moulton range rationalised. BMC take full control of all Moulton mass production.
1967 Moulton Bicycles Limited sold to Raleigh and Alex Moulton retained as consultant.
1970 Colin Martin rides prototype 'Mk III' to Australia. Raleigh launch Moulton 'Mk III'.
1974 Raleigh cease production of the Moulton bicycle.
1977 'Cycling' reports Alex Moulton working on new bicycle.
1980 'Sunday Times' reports existence of Moulton Preservation and Moulton Bicycle Club.
1983 Scheduled launch of new Alex Moulton bicycle.

B) DO's and DON'Ts

It is assumed that the reader is familiar with the adjustment and maintenance of the individual conventional components of the Moulton. If not it is recommended that a conventional bicycle maintenance book is studied to cover these points. The following is a list of points to bear in mind when using the Moulton. Many of these hints are based on those in the original Moulton instruction leaflet.

DO's

1) DO ensure that the saddle height is correctly adjusted. If several riders are to use the bicycle regularly the relative seat positions should be marked on the pillar e.g. by a light mark with a hack saw. (This suggestion has been criticised as being vandalistic. On earlier Moultons the seat pillar tended to get scored and scratched quite easily and a small, neat saw mark would not be a great disfigurement but if you are concerned for the appearance of your machine, try a neat mark with a waterproof marker pen).
2) DO mount the Moulton by stepping through the frame. This is safer than 'scooting' and puts less strain on the cranks and suspension.
3) DO use the lowest gear which you can comfortably pedal.
4) DO ensure that the Sturmey-Archer gear, where fitted is correctly adjusted. With three-speeds set the gear selector to middle gear and adjust the cable length by using the knurled connector and locknut. The indicator rod can be viewed through a circular opening in the right-hand (offside) wheelnut. The end of the indicator rod should be exactly level with the end of the hub spindle. With four speeds the same procedure is adopted but the indicator rod is viewed through the left-hand wheelnut with the selector set for gear No. 2. In both cases the control cable should be in good condition, well lubricated and free of kinks and unnecessary or extreme changes of direction.
5) DO make sure that the tyres are inflated hard. (See Appendix C) Rims and Tyres). This cannot be over emphasised.
6) DO ensure that the front wheel is fitted with the adjustable cone on the left-hand side of the machine (as viewed when riding it). Make sure that the wheel spindle is fully home in the fork ends.
7) DO check that the fork clearance either side of the rear wheel is equal.
8) DO make sure that the chain is adjusted to give a slackness midway of approximately ¾".
9) DO check the overall wheel alignment after adjusting or replacing a wheel by turning the bicycle upside down and running a straight edge along both sides of the rear wheel. If correctly aligned the straight edge should touch either side of the front wheel. An extruded aluminium 'L' or box section from a D.I.Y. store makes a suitable straight edge if sufficiently rigid.
10) DO ensure, when reassembling a 'Stowaway', that the main beam joint is fully home and then tightened with the Allen Key, as the joint is very easily damaged if ridden when slack. If there is any evidence of 'belling' of the main beam tubing at the joint do not ride the machine.
11) DO check any new rattle as soon as it starts and make a regular check of bolt tightness and bearing adjustment.

12) DO regularly clean and lubricate the bicycle.
13) DO make sure that, if the front brake bolt has been removed the short bush through which it passes (situated in the front fork crown) is not displaced as this bush holds the coil spring and rubber column of the front suspension. (If your machine was built in or after 1965 it will probably not have this bush fitted, hence the coil spring, rubber column and abutment will spring out on removal of the brake bolt – unless you pass in a 'keeper', such as a screwdriver blade, as you remove the brake).
14) DO ensure that the rubber bellows of the front suspension are correctly fitted and free of splits as any dust or grit passing through to the suspension splines may cause serious damage to the suspension.

DON'TS

1) DON'T ride 'Hands Off'. The low flywheel effect of the 16" wheel, the small rake of the steering and short relative length of front tyre in contact with the road render this a hazardous exercise, as well as a pointless one.
2) DON'T hang shopping bags on the handlebars as the light steering is badly affected by such free-hanging loads.
3) DON'T exceed the recommended carrier loads of 50 lbs. for the rear carrier and 20 lbs. for the front.
4) DON'T allow oil to come into contact with the rubber suspension components as this will cause deterioration. This is particularly important now that spares are in short supply. (Molybdenum grease may be used on the front suspension splines and on the rubber column/coil spring assembly. Also, according to its manufacturers, LPS 1 aerosol lubricant will not harm rubber).
5) DON'T abuse the machine by riding it up and down pavement kerbs or similar obstacles.

C) RIMS AND TYRES

Most countries, including those which have long used the metric system, identify bicycle tyre sizes by using imperial units. Do not imagine though that just because a tyre is labelled 16 x 1 3/8" it will fit your standard Moulton rim. There are Polish and Italian tyres thus marked which will not, and there is a similarly useless French 16 x 1 3/8" x 1¼". I once spent a very frustrating half-hour on a Flemish roadside trying to fit a Belgian 16 x 1 3/8" x 1½" tyre to my Moulton!

The problem is that all these sizes are nominal, the large figure being the nominal outer tyre diameter. The *critical* dimensions are the bead seat diameter and, to a lesser extent, the width. These 'ETRTO' figures are now given on many tyres and it is to be hoped that they will be universally adopted in the near future. They are given in millimeters, usually within brackets.

The mass produced Moultons used the E3J rim for 16" wheeled machines and the E2J for 14".

i) 16 x 1 3/8" Format. The E3J rim is usually only available in Britain in steel. Early Moultons had 36 hole rims but later a 28 hole standard was adopted. E3J rims are also currently available with 20 holes, these being primarily intended for juvenile use. A high quality 9 oz. special Weinmann 36 hole E3J alloy rim has been produced for Fomac Incorporated of the U.S.A. and is available from them for around 15 dollars (1981 price – see Chapter 2 notes for address).

The correct 'ETRTO' tyre figures for E3J rims are 32–349 to 37–349 where the first figure is the tyre width and the second the bead seat diameter. The original Moulton tyres were made by Dunlop and were all 37–349's. There was an amber walled Sprite, designed to run at 70 p.s.i. and a black utility version of the same tyre, designed to run at 50–60 p.s.i. (The instructions varied from time to time). Early versions were cotton corded but tended to fail prematurely because of the fabric 'laddering', leading to bulging and puncturing. Later versions were nylon corded and marked accordingly. These tyres held the road well, rolled easily and the tread lasted a long time.

About 1972 Dunlop ceased production of all bicycle tyres and subsequently a very similar black ribbed tyre was made by Raleigh in Poland. This was called the 'Raleigh S.W Nylon' and was designed to run at 55 p.s.i. but has now been discontinued. It is worth looking out for the Dunlop and Raleigh tyres as they are generally better than most currently produced tyres and they still turn up from time to time. (Raleigh currently produce a white wall 16 x 1 3/8" juvenile tyre called the 'Record').

Another possibility for the E3J rim is the Clement 16 x *1¼"* (Italian nomenclature) juvenile tyre. This is a lightly ribbed narrow section tyre which is apparently produced in black, white and gumwall (amber wall) versions. The first two options are listed by Falcon in the U.K.

The most commonly available tyre in Britain which will fit the E3J rim is the Michelin Universal, which is available in black or white. The recommended pressure is 45 p.s.i. but the tyre does not seem to quibble at up to 70 p.s.i. The carcass rarely distorts in the way that the earlier Dunlop tyres did but the tread rubber is quite soft. Consequently tyre wear is relatively rapid and I find that the tyre tends to puncture in the wet rather more than one would expect. On the other hand the Michelins were always about 25% cheaper than the purpose-made Dunlops.

Recently a number of imported E3J tyres have come onto the U.K. market, mostly from the Far East. These include Kenda and Leo (both nylon corded). Pagoda and Trelleborg, the latter being Swedish. I have only limited experience of these tyres but I understand that the Kenda wears well although the side walls tend to fail before the tread wears out. The Leo seems to be prone to early carcass failure and to have a high rolling resistance.

It is interesting to compare the widths of different tyres on the same rim. The Dunlop and Michelin both measure little more than 1¼" whereas the Kenda is almost 1½"; all are nominally 1 3/8"!

ii) 14 x 1 3/8" Format. The E2J rim was used for 14" wheel Moultons. This is usually only available in steel in the U.K. but the 'Mini Automatic' had alloy rims. Both 28 and 20 hole steel rims are available, the latter being intended primarily for juvenile use. The original Dunlop black ribbed Sprite based 14 x 1 3/8" tyre is no longer available nor is the Dunlop block treaded utility tyre used on some 'Minis'. Suitable Michelin Universals, in black or white, are readily available and compatible tyres are likely to be imported by the firms mentioned in the previous paragraph. The ETRTO code range for the E2J rim is 32–298 to 37–298 and it seems likely that Clement produce a 14 x *1¼*" (Italian nomenclature) lightweight juvenile tyre which would fit.

iii) 17 x 1¼" Format. The Dunlop 1¼" high pressure racing tyre, specially developed for the Moulton, was originally described as 16 x 1¼" (ETRTO code 32–369) but as it had a greater overall diameter than the 16 x 1 3/8" (which in any case is nearer 16½") it was later reclassified as 17 x 1¼". This is a unique format, the only rims which fit being those specially made for the Moulton (originally by Dunlop and Milremo). Just to confuse the issue there is a Swedish 17 x 1¼" format but this is incompatible, the ETRTO code being 32–357.

Supplies of the Moulton 17 x 1¼" tyre and rim have been very scarce for some years but this format will be used on the new Alex Moulton bicycle and hence, from sometime in 1982, fresh supplies should be available. It is believed that the tyres and rims will both be of better quality than hitherto.

In the meantime if you have a 17 x 1¼" cover but cannot obtain the correct inner tube, a standard Michelin 16 x 1 3/8" tube will suffice. This cannot be obtained with a Presta valve but you can use the Woods valve version if you very carefully ream out the valve hole in the rim. Alternatively you can unscrew the whole valve assembly from the tube and screw on a Presta valve body.

iv) 17" Sprint Format. The original tubular tyres and matching Milremo sprint rims were supplied by Anglo Continental Cycles and Accessories (Ron Kitching) of Harrogate. I have been told by Kitchings that they can supply tubulars of this format to special order and I understand that these may be made by Barum of Czechoslovakia. The original tubulars were described as 16 x 1¼" No. 5's. Roger Piper, of California, has ascertained that the original Moulton sprint rim was identical to that used on scaled-down racing bicycles made for young children by both Legnano and Frejus about ten years ago. These juvenile sprints were made by Nisi and Fiamme whereas the tyres were made by Atlanta Gumma who own the D'Alessandro trademark. I understand that The Holdsworthy Company Limited are the U.K. distributors for all three brands but the company was unable to give any further information about these rims or tyres.

Later Moulton sprint rims were made by Scheeren in 24 spoke versions for rear wheels and 20 spoke versions for the front. The later tubulars were marked up as *18"* (although they are nearer to 16½" diameter). These tyres were Milremo 'Records' and a 'Junior' 18" tubular by the same maker is listed in the current (1982) Ron Kitching catalogue (p.137).

Anyone who wishes to research the various tyre formats in greater detail is advised to peruse 'Sutherland's Handbook for Bicycle Mechanics', 3rd Edition. (Available from Ron Kitching by whose kind permission the spoke chart below is reproduced).

v) Spoke Chart for Moulton Wheels.

(This chart only gives the most frequently encountered spoke configurations).

Rim Size (All 28 hole)	**TYPE OF HUB** Front	Rear	Rear Derailleur	S.A. Hub or Duomatic	GH6 Dynohub
14 x 1 3/8"	5 7/16"	5 5/16"		5 1/8"	5 7/16–4 13/16"
16 x 1 3/8"	6 5/16"	6 7/32"		6"	6 5/16–5 11/16"
17" HP	6 13/16"	6 11/16"	6¾"	6½"	6 13/16–6 1/8"
17" Sprint	7 1/8"	7"	7"	6¾"	

NB: Spoke lengths are measured in inches from the inside bend of the head to the end of the spoke.

Use 1/16" longer spoke for HP rims that are not depressed at the spoke holes.

Use 1/16" shorter spoke on the driving side of wheels dished for multiple freewheel.

D) MAIN PATENTS

The Moulton bicycle, in whole and in part, was patented in many countries including the U.S.S.R. The main British Patents were as follows:

British Patent Number	**Brief Description**	**Corresponding U.S. Patent**
907467	The original Moulton bicycle concept	3083038 + 9
909446 1047783	) Front End)	3208767
1081425	Rear Carrier	
1086638	Frame	
1202886	Freewheel (very small cogged)	
1205286	Mk 3 Rear End	
Other U.S. Patents:	3151878 Suspension 3220748 Frame	

Many other Patents were applied for but not taken out or granted. The Moulton is also the subject of certain Registered Designs.

E) GEARING

1) Hub Gears

This section includes gear tables for the hub gears most likely to be found in use on Moulton bicycles. These gears are as follows:

i) Sturmey-Archer Gears

AW – This is the standard British wide ratio three speed hub, the most successful of its type in the world. It gives direct drive with an upward shift of 33 1/3% and a downward shift of 25%. The AW was introduced in 1936 and is still in production. It was original equipment on some Moulton bicycles including 'Series One' 'Standards' and the 'Minx'. The S3C is the version of this gear with integral coaster brake. The S3B is an AW with cable-operated hub brake. (The S3B was original equipment on mass produced 'Mk III's'). There is also a version of the AW combined with a Dynohub. This is known as the AG.

FW – This was the wide ratio four speed hub, introduced in 1946 and discontinued in 1968. The majority of mass produced Moultons were equipped with this gear which gives direct drive with an upward shift of 26.6% and downward shifts of 21.1% and 33 1/3%. The FG was an FW combined with a Dynohub.

S5 – This is the wide ratio five speed hub which gives the same gearing as the FW with an additional upward shift of 50%. It requires two changers, the right hand operating as a three-speed, the left as an 'overdrive' to bring in the 'Super High' and 'Super Low' gears.
The S5 was never fitted as original equipment but it is very suitable for Moulton use especially as it enables a very high gear to be achieved without using a very large chainwheel. Furthermore FW gears can be converted to S5 specification.
The gear was introduced in 1966 and is still in production although not advertised in the U.K. Early versions employed a bell-crank for the left hand changer coupling at the hub whereas later units are fitted with a pull-chain to match the right hand coupling. Jack Lauterwasser has evolved a third system (see note below on converting four-speeds).

ii) Fichtel & Sachs Gears

Torpedo-Duomatic – This is the two speed back-pedal brake which was original equipment on the 'Automatic', Mini Automatic', 'S Stowaway' and later M5 'Stowaways'. Gear change is effected by slightly back-pedalling and hence no cable is required and the gear cannot go out of adjustment. The Duomatic gives direct drive and a 36% upward shift. It is still in production. Similar units have been produced by Shimano (Japan) and Bendix (U.S.A.).
The Torpedo-Automatic is similar to the Duomatic but the gear change is effected by an integral centrifugal mechanism when a certain wheel revolution rate is achieved.

NB: Three-speed wide ratio hub gears are also produced by Fichtel & Sachs, Shimano and Puch.

iii) Hub Gear Tables

The following tables give gearing options obtainable by using the standard 52 tooth chainwheel. The gears are expressed in inches (see explanation in Chapter 8) and are based on the nominal wheel sizes. As a point of reference single speed bicycles are usually fitted with gears of 60–68".

Wheel Diameter	Gear	Sprocket Teeth	1st	2nd	3rd	4th	5th
14"	S-A AW & Derivatives	13	42	56	75		
		14	39	52	69		
		15	36	49	65		
14"	S-A FW & S5 (5th gear in parenthesis applies only to S5)	13	37	44	56	71	(84)
		14	35	41	52	66	(78)
		15	33	39	49	62	(74)
		16	30	36	46	57	(68)
14"	F & S Duomatic	13	56	76			
		14	52	71			
		15	49	66			
		16	46	62			
		17	43	58			
16"	S-A AW & Derivatives	13	48	64	85		
		14	45	59	79		
		15	42	55	74		
		16	39	52	69		
16"	S-A FW & S5 (5th gear in parenthesis applies only to S5)	13	43	51	64	81	(96)
		14	40	47	59	75	(89)
		15	37	44	55	70	(83)
	Cyclo 3-speed Derailleur converter giving 15 speeds with S5 gear	16	35	41	52	66	(78)
		19	29	35	44	55	(66)
		23	24	29	36	46	(54)
16"	F & S Duomatic	13	64	87			
		14	59	81			
		15	55	75			
		16	52	71			
		17	49	67			
		18	46	63			
		19	44	60			

Wheel Diameter	Gear	Sprocket Teeth	1st	2nd	3rd	4th	5th
17"	S-A AW & Derivatives	13	51	68	91		
		14	47	63	84		
		15	44	59	79		
		16	41	55	74		
17"	S-A FW & S5 (5th gear in parenthesis applies only to S5)	13	45	54	68	86	(102)
		14	42	50	63	80	(95)
		15	39	46	59	75	(88)
	Cyclo 3-speed Derailleur converter giving 15 speeds with S5 gear	16	37	44	55	70	(83)
		19	31	37	47	59	(70)
		23	26	30	38	49	(58)
17"	F & S Duomatic	13	68	93			
		14	63	86			
		15	59	80			
		16	55	75			
		17	52	71			
		18	49	67			
		19	47	63			
		20	44	60			

iv) **Further Information on Hub Gears** – Both Sturmey-Archer and Fichtel & Sachs produce very informative brochures and leaflets on their current hub gears. Sturmey-Archer are also very helpful in giving details of obsolete gears such as the FW and the medium and close ratio three and four speed hubs.

v) **Spares for Obsolete Hubs** – Most parts which are subject to wear (such as bearings) are common to current gears and many S5 parts can be used in the FW. One of the commonest reasons for an obsolete hub gear becoming inoperative is damage to the toggle, coupling and indicator rod. Sid Standard of Beeston can usually supply these parts for the old four speed gears and, if the problem is merely a broken toggle chain, any competent cycle repairer should be able to rivet on the chain section of an AW coupling.

It is also possible to convert some obsolete hub gears to operate with an AW coupling. (I have an AM medium ratio hub thus modified). Jack Lauterwasser may be able to carry out such modifications for interested Moulton owners.

vi) Interchangeability of Sturmey-Archer Hubs – Many of these gears (but not all) are interchangeable. For instance, the S5, AW, FW and AM can all be used in the same hub shell. This is very useful because a new rear wheel is not necessarily required if you wish to change to a different type of hub gear.

vii) Sprocket Sizes – Sturmey-Archer and Fichtel & Sachs three lugged sprockets are interchangeable (as are Shimano, Puch and several coaster brake manufacturers' sprockets). Sturmey sprockets range in size from 13 through to 20 and 22 tooth. Fichtel & Sachs make 14 to 22 tooth and also make a 12 tooth sprocket which is marketed solely for use with the Torpedo-Jet coaster brake. The spacer washers used with hub gear sprockets are too large to permit the chain to wrap round the latter sprocket correctly but, if this problem could be overcome, the 12 tooth cog could be used with hub gears. (Remember that Moultons produced their own 11 tooth hub gear sprocket for John Woodburn).

The 12 tooth sprocket is not imported into the U.K. but can be supplied direct by the German factory in batches of 10 at 75p each. (1981 price). It can be fitted to the Perry Coaster B500 hub used on the 'Continental' and early 'Stowaways' in order to give a 69" gear.

F & S sprockets from 16–22 tooth are dished as are S–A sprockets from 16–20 and 22 tooth. The S–A 14 tooth sprocket has been produced in dished form but currently appears to be made only in the flat version. 3/32" S–A sprockets can be obtained from Morris Vulcan (Sales) Ltd., who make the Bickerton cycle. (Normally they are 1/8").

viii) Conversion of Sturmey-Archer Four Speeds to Five Speed Operation
As explained in Chapter 5, inside every four speed hub is a five-speed trying to get out. This conversion is not recommended by the makers, no doubt for product liability and commercial reasons, and certainly should not be attempted by the unskilled. However, in the right hands the conversion works extremely well as I can vouch from personal experience.

Jack Lauterwasser will generally be able to carry out this work to any Sturmey-Archer four-speed hub in reasonably good condition (except those fitted with integral Dynohubs) for approximately £4 (1981 price) plus postage and packing. This does not include provision of the second control cable, trigger or cable stop (fulcrum clip) which are standard items. Jack has recently evolved a unique left hand changer coupling which is extremely smooth in operation and has a quick-release cable attachment.

ix) Derailleur Converters for Hub Gears – These consist of multiple sprockets attached to a hub gear to give a wider choice of gearing. Thus a three speed derailleur allied with a five speed hub gear will give fifteen gears although it will not usually be possible to select all fifteen in sequence. Furthermore some gears may be so close that they are effectively the same (i.e. within 2").

The following converters are available;

Cyclo – This firm once made a two-speed converter (13 + 15T) specifically for use with the Moulton as did Gian Robert. Cyclo still make converters but the only unit suitable for Moulton use is the three-speed (16 – 19 – 23T) which can give useful touring ratios if used with an S5 hub gear. (See bracketed sections of S5 gear tables).

Cyclo converters are designed for use with the original chainwheel and 1/8" chain. The multiple sprocket unit simply clips on to the gear in place of the usual single sprocket. A compact but robust rear changer mechanism is required and I have found the Huret Allvit suitable. Some 1/8" chains work perfectly well with this gear but the rivet width of 1/8" chains varies quite considerably so this is a point worth checking (but note that some cycle dealers will tell you, incorrectly, that no 1/8" chain will work with a modern rear derailleur changer). The standard chain will need about ten additional links to run around the changer mechanism and the removable spring link should be dispensed with for smoother running. Consequently, purchase of a suitable riveter/rivet extractor is recommended (e.g. the Cyclo Rivoli).

Some filing of the rear mechanism hanger plate will probably be necessary in order to fit it to the standard Moulton rear forks and the hanger plate retaining bolt may not fit. This may present a problem if you often need to remove the rear wheel and a brazed-on hanger plate would be a possible solution.

Ernest Rogers – This Californian bicycle engineer produces limited numbers of a special driver unit for Sturmey-Archer hubs which will accept no less than five Regina 3/32" Derailleur sprockets. It is then necessary to use a 6 5/16" axle for the Sturmey-Archer gear and the standard rear forks will require some springing out. This could be difficult (but not impossible) with 'Series Two' forks which are very rigid.

The Rogers unit basically consists of a Regina outer block brazed on to a sawn-off Sturmey-Archer driver.

The brazing is a possible disadvantage but the unit is fairly cheap (about £10 plus cost of sprockets in 1981) and has the advantage of wide gearing options and the use of a modern 3/32" low friction chain. This will, however, necessitate not only a new chain, sprockets and rear mechanism but also a new chainset.

Danish Converter – A special driver for Sturmey-Archer gears which will accept four 3/32" Sun Tour Winner sprockets (15 – 30T) is produced in Denmark. It is quite a costly unit (about £22 including postage in 1981), the sprockets being extra. As far as I know no brazing is involved but it is probable that a long axle would be required for the hub gear. Otherwise the advantages and disadvantages are broadly as for the Rogers unit.

The Danish converter appears to be reliable having been used by

Scandinavian cyclists for a round-the-world tour. The unit can be obtained via Finn Wodschow of Copenhagen.

Other Units – From time to time limited numbers of other 3/32" converters are produced by certain bicycle engineers. One of these uses Maillard sprockets with the obsolete Sturmey-Archer threaded sprocket driver units. According to D.W. Naylor, a Moulton owner from Workington, these drivers will accept a pair of standard fixed wheel sprockets in which case no further conversion is required. (See letter to 'Cycletouring', October 1981).

2) **Derailleur Gears**

i) **Mechanics** – The main requirement for a rear changer mechanism for use with the Moulton is that it should be compact for maximum chain wrapround and ground clearance. A large sprocket capacity is desirable but mechanisms with long touring arms are not suitable. The Simplex Racing gear has been used in the past but can give rather vague gear changes unless kept extremely clean and well adjusted. The current recommended gear, in the medium price range, is the Sun Tour Superbe.

Front changer mechanisms will almost invariably require special fixing modifications as the standard units will not fit the Moulton seat tube.

When fitting a derailleur mechanism to standard Moulton rear forks (i.e. other than those built expressly to accept derailleur gears) it is advisable to have a hanger plate or boss brazed on. The forks will also need to be sprung out and this may be difficult (but not impossible) with the 'Series Two' type.

ii) **Chainsets** – Modern derailleurs use 3/32" chains and hence the 1/8" chainset (i.e. cranks, chainwheel, axle and fittings) will need replacement. With 'Mk III's" the bottom bracket will almost certainly need to be cut down and rethreaded because most good quality cotterless chainsets cannot be fitted to the Raleigh type bottom bracket.

Very large chainwheels are required for use with all derailleur geared Moultons. Most manufacturers produce a 52 tooth chainwheel but sizes above this can be hard to obtain. Milremo, Polchlopek and Sun Tour produce 54 tooth chainwheels whereas Tevano and Zeus make 56 tooth types. The best bet for the Moulton is probably a T.A. chainwheel. These can be obtained in up to 68 tooth sizes and larger sizes have been made to special order. In order to clear the rear suspension pivot do not exceed 66 teeth on standard 'Series One and Two' frames.

iii) **Sprockets** – In the past Moultons have produced a successful 9 tooth prototype derailleur sprocket but the smallest size on most commonly available five speed blocks is 14 tooth; with six speed blocks, 13 tooth and with seven speeds, 12 tooth. Some ranges, usually the more expensive ones, offer smaller sprockets e.g. the Shimano Freehub goes down to 11 teeth.

iv) **Derailleur Gear Tables** – These were prepared by Paul Cooper of the Moulton Bicycle Club and cover the nominal 16" and 17" wheel sizes.

GEAR TABLE FOR 16" WHEELS

No. of Teeth on Rear Sprocket	No. of Teeth on Chainwheel															
	44	46	48	50	52	54	56	58	60	62	64	66	68	70	72	74
11	64.0	66.9	69.8	72.7	75.6	78.5	81.5	84.4	87.3	90.2	93.1	96.0	98.9	101.8	104.7	107.6
12	58.7	61.3	64.0	66.7	69.3	72.0	74.7	77.3	80.0	82.7	85.3	88.0	90.7	93.3	96.0	98.7
13	54.2	56.6	59.1	61.5	64.0	66.5	68.9	71.4	73.8	76.3	78.8	81.2	83.7	86.2	88.6	91.1
14	50.3	52.6	54.9	57.1	59.4	61.7	64.0	66.3	68.6	70.9	73.1	75.4	77.7	80.0	82.3	84.6
15	46.9	49.1	51.2	53.3	55.5	57.6	59.7	61.9	64.0	66.1	68.3	70.4	72.5	74.7	76.8	78.9
16	44.0	46.0	48.0	50.0	52.0	54.0	56.0	58.0	60.0	62.0	64.0	66.0	68.0	70.0	72.0	74.0
17	41.4	43.3	45.2	47.1	48.9	50.8	52.7	54.6	56.5	58.4	60.2	62.1	64.0	65.9	67.8	69.6
18	39.1	40.9	42.7	44.4	46.2	48.0	49.8	51.6	53.3	55.1	56.9	58.7	60.4	62.2	64.0	65.8
19	37.1	38.7	40.4	42.1	43.8	45.5	47.2	48.8	50.5	52.2	53.9	55.6	57.3	58.9	60.6	62.3
20	35.2	36.8	38.4	40.0	41.6	43.2	44.8	46.4	48.0	49.6	51.2	52.8	54.4	56.0	57.6	59.2
21	33.5	35.0	36.6	38.1	39.6	41.1	42.7	44.2	45.7	47.2	48.8	50.3	51.8	53.3	54.9	56.4
22	32.0	33.5	34.9	36.4	37.8	39.3	40.7	42.2	43.6	45.1	46.5	48.0	49.5	50.9	52.4	53.8
23	30.6	32.0	33.4	34.8	36.2	37.6	39.0	40.3	41.7	43.1	44.5	45.9	47.3	48.7	50.1	51.5
24	29.3	30.7	32.0	33.3	34.7	36.0	37.3	38.7	40.0	41.3	42.7	44.0	45.3	46.7	48.0	49.3
25	28.2	29.4	30.7	32.0	33.3	34.6	35.8	37.1	38.4	39.7	41.0	42.2	43.5	44.8	46.1	47.4
26	27.1	28.3	29.5	30.8	32.0	33.2	34.5	35.7	36.9	38.2	39.4	40.6	41.8	43.1	44.3	45.5
27	26.1	27.3	28.4	29.6	30.8	32.0	33.2	34.4	35.6	36.7	37.9	39.1	40.3	41.5	42.7	43.9
28	25.1	26.3	27.4	28.6	29.7	30.9	32.0	33.1	34.3	35.4	36.6	37.7	38.9	40.0	41.1	42.3
29	24.3	25.4	26.5	27.6	28.7	29.8	30.9	32.0	33.1	34.2	35.3	36.4	37.5	38.6	39.7	40.8
30	23.5	24.5	25.6	26.7	27.7	28.8	29.9	30.9	32.0	33.1	34.1	35.2	36.3	37.3	38.4	39.5

GEAR TABLE FOR 17" WHEELS

No. of Teeth on Rear Sprocket	No. of Teeth on Chainwheel															
	44	46	48	50	52	54	56	58	60	62	64	66	68	70	72	74
9	83.1	86.9	90.7	94.4	98.2	102.0	105.8	109.6	113.3	117.1	120.9	124.7	128.4	132.2	136.0	139.8
10	74.8	78.2	81.6	85.0	88.4	91.8	95.2	98.6	102.0	105.4	108.8	112.2	115.6	119.0	122.4	125.8
11	68.0	71.1	74.2	77.3	80.4	83.5	86.5	89.6	92.7	95.8	98.9	102.0	105.1	108.2	111.3	114.4
12	62.3	65.2	68.0	70.8	73.7	76.5	79.3	82.2	85.0	87.8	90.7	93.5	96.3	99.2	102.0	104.8
13	57.5	60.2	62.8	65.4	68.0	70.6	73.2	75.8	78.5	81.1	83.7	86.3	88.9	91.5	94.2	96.8
14	53.4	55.9	58.3	60.7	63.1	65.6	68.0	70.4	72.9	75.3	77.7	80.1	82.6	85.0	87.4	89.9
15	49.9	52.1	54.4	56.7	58.9	61.2	63.5	65.7	68.0	70.3	72.5	74.8	77.1	79.3	81.6	83.9
16	46.8	48.9	51.0	53.1	55.3	57.4	59.5	61.6	63.8	65.9	68.0	70.1	72.3	74.4	76.5	78.6
17	44.0	46.0	48.0	50.0	52.0	54.0	56.0	58.0	60.0	62.0	64.0	66.0	68.0	70.0	72.0	74.0
18	41.6	43.4	45.3	47.2	49.1	51.0	52.9	54.8	56.7	58.6	60.4	62.3	64.2	66.1	68.0	69.9
19	39.4	41.2	42.9	44.7	46.5	48.3	50.1	51.9	53.7	55.5	57.3	59.1	60.8	62.6	64.4	66.2
20	37.4	39.1	40.8	42.5	44.2	45.9	47.6	49.3	51.0	52.7	54.4	56.1	57.8	59.5	61.2	62.9
21	35.6	37.2	38.9	40.5	42.1	43.7	45.3	47.0	48.6	50.2	51.8	53.4	55.0	56.7	58.3	59.9
22	34.0	35.5	37.1	38.6	40.2	41.7	43.3	44.8	46.4	47.9	49.5	51.0	52.5	54.1	55.6	57.2
23	32.5	34.0	35.5	37.0	38.4	39.9	41.4	42.9	44.3	45.8	47.3	48.8	50.3	51.7	53.2	54.7
24	31.2	32.6	34.0	35.4	36.8	38.2	39.7	41.1	42.5	43.9	45.3	46.7	48.2	49.6	51.0	52.4
25	29.9	31.3	32.6	34.0	35.4	36.7	38.1	39.4	40.8	42.2	43.5	44.9	46.2	47.6	49.0	50.3
26	28.8	30.1	31.4	32.7	34.0	35.3	36.6	37.9	39.2	40.5	41.8	43.2	44.5	45.8	47.1	48.4
27	27.7	29.0	30.2	31.5	32.7	34.0	35.3	36.5	37.8	39.0	40.3	41.5	42.8	44.1	45.3	46.6
28	26.7	27.9	29.1	30.4	31.6	32.8	34.0	35.2	36.4	37.6	38.9	40.1	41.3	42.5	43.7	44.9
29	25.8	27.0	28.1	29.3	30.5	31.7	32.8	34.0	35.2	36.3	37.5	38.7	39.9	41.0	42.2	43.4
30	24.9	26.1	27.2	28.3	29.5	30.6	31.7	32.9	34.0	35.1	36.3	37.4	38.5	39.7	40.8	41.9
31	24.1	25.2	26.3	27.4	28.5	29.6	30.7	31.8	32.9	34.0	35.1	36.2	37.3	38.4	39.5	40.6

F) FAULTS PECULIAR TO THE MOULTON

1) Front Suspension

a) **Squeak** – It is quite easy to remove the main coil spring and rubber column in order to clean off any traces of corrosion and then regrease the assembly including the spring abutment. This will usually eliminate any tendency of the front suspension to squeak.

Only molybdenum grease such as Molyslip should be used because oil based products will attack the rubber suspension medium. It seems that some dealers tried to cure front suspension squeaks by turning the bicycle upside down and pouring oil down the suspension splines in direct contravention of the maker's instructions. No doubt they still blamed the manufacturer when the front suspension later went soft!

To lubricate the front suspension proceed as follows;

1) Turn the bicycle upside down and remove the front wheel.

2) Remove the front mudguard (or release it from the brake bolt – leaving the bolt in position – and swing the mudguard clear of the opening in the underside of the fork crown).

3) Firmly hold the crown of the forks placing your thumb over the opening in the underside of the crown (which houses the spring abutment). Now withdraw the brake bolt. If your machine is not fitted with a brake bush, the abutment will now be loose and can spring out (which is why your thumb is over it!).

Early machines (generally pre-1965) usually have a brake bush which retains the abutment during removal of the front brake. If yours is one of these, it will now be necessary to also remove this before the abutment will spring out.

4) Having removed the abutment, push down the forks and withdraw the coil spring and rubber column for greasing.

5) Reverse steps 1) – 4) to reassemble.

b) **Play** – First check that the play is in the steering and not in the wheel bearings. Next, check that the bottom nylon bearing retaining ring (inside rubber bellows) is not loose. If it is, tighten with a 'C' spanner. If the play is still apparent remove the handlebar stem, and, using a long-handled, small-headed Phillips screwdriver, tighten up the rebound stop retaining screw if found necessary (on early models and late Raleigh-built bikes a normal screwdriver slot head is fitted).

(It is vitally important to use the correct screwdriver for any work involving removal of the rebound stop. Many hardware stores will tell you that a suitably long but small-headed Phillips screwdriver cannot be obtained. Not so! Ask them to order you a Stanley 64–592 2pt. The correct tool may mean the difference between success and failure).

If play is still apparent more drastic action is required.

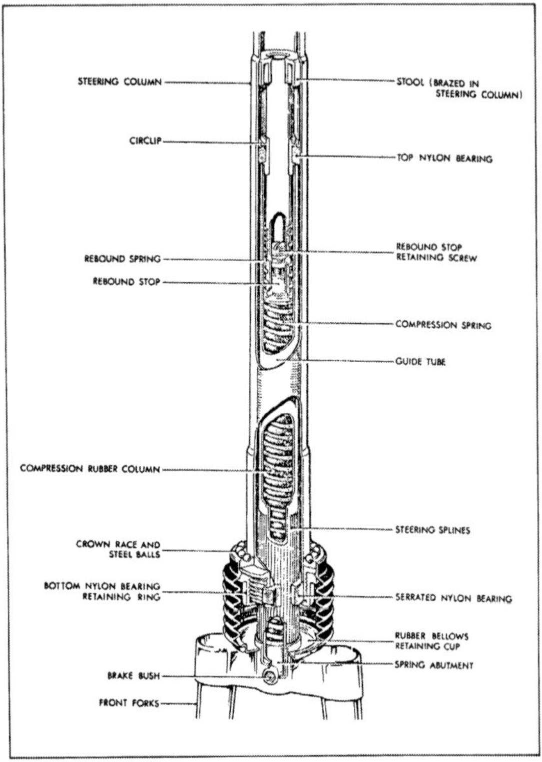

Cutaway drawing of front suspension.

Usually the cause is a worn serrated nylon bearing. This item is in very short supply although Alex Moulton Limited may be able to supply a replacement from their small stockpile. Before contacting them count the number of splines as this changed at various stages of production.

The first Moultons had 36 splined nylon bearings with a nominal diameter of 7/8". About the beginning of 1964 the diameter was increased to 1". In 1969 the number of splines was reduced to 24. The 'Mini' and its derivatives also had a 24 splined bearing, this having a nominal diameter of 7/8".

There is also a plain nylon bearing at the top of the guide tube. The size of this varies, those for the 'Mini' range and very early 'Series One' machines being smaller.

The front suspension may be dismantled in the following manner (based on official Moulton instructions to dealers);

1) Remove fork – with front brake stirrup attached – from the machine in the conventional manner.

2) Remove top end of rubber bellows from fork crown race.

3) Remove brake bolt (and where fitted push out brake bush) from fork crown and drop out spring abutment, together with compression spring and compression rubber column from inside the guide tube, through the opening under the fork crown. Whilst doing this it is advisable to hold your thumb firmly over the opening under the crown in order to stop the abutment flying out. Slight pressure on the underside of the abutment may aid removal of the brake bolt etc.

4) Unscrew rebound stop retaining screw with a long Phillips screwdriver inserted in the top of the steering column (or conventional screwdriver for earlier models and late Raleigh-built machines).

5) Unscrew bottom nylon bearing retaining ring and separate the steering column from the forks and guide tube with a strong pull.

6) The rebound stop and rebound spring can then be removed from the guide tube.

7) Remove circlip from top of guide tube – pull off top nylon (plain) bearing, serrated nylon bearing, retaining ring and bellows-retaining cup.

Reassemble in the reverse order using a smear of Molyslip or other molybdenum grease on steering splines and both nylon bearings. If rust is found on steel splines, remove with wire brush before reassembling. If difficulty is experienced in replacing rebound stop and rebound stop retaining screw, a little plasticine used in the screw head slots will hold the piece on the end of the screwdriver while inserting. Ensure that the pin in the rebound stop engages in the locating slots inside the guide tube.

As previously stated it is often very difficult to obtain a suitably long Phillips screwdriver with a fine enough head. Even with the right tool it may prove very difficult to budge a fifteen year old rebound stop retaining screw. If you can find a very small diameter impact screwdriver this may solve the problem. If in doubt contact Alex Moulton Limited for advice rather than ruin your suspension unit.

On one occasion I had to resort to drilling off the head of the screw to dismantle the suspension. Despite taking every precaution I succeeded in drilling out not only the screw head but the whole screw and seating. I improvised a repair using a 3/8" diameter flat-headed bolt in lieu of the rebound stop. This passed right up inside the stool (which normally holds the rebound stop assembly) and was retained by dropping a spacer sleeve (cut from ½" stainless steel tubing) and a serrated locking washer over the threaded end of the bolt, followed by the nut which was 'stirred' on until tight using a large conventional screwdriver. Although not 'factory approved' this repair appears to have worked well. However, repairs to the front suspension should not be undertaken lightly.

D. Brian Williams of Toronto has evolved an alternative solution to the problem of dismantling recalcitrant front suspension units. The Phillips screw head had been mistaken for a straight slot and irrevocably damaged. Brian solved the problem by drilling an accurately positioned hole right through the side of the steering column, guide tube and stool tube and thus drilled the rebound stop retaining screw into two parts.

This is possible because there is an open portion of bolt shank above the rebound stop. Very accurate drilling is required but the consecutive tubes tend to prevent the drill bit from wandering. A spare spoke is used to determine the position of the rebound stop, which is then marked on the outside of the steering column. It is then necessary to drill far enough above this point to clear the rebound stop but below the seating for the head of the retaining screw. It is therefore necessary to ascertain these dimensions before proceeding further.

It is advisable to drill a small pilot hole first and then follow up with one a little larger than the retaining screw diameter. Any resulting metal swarf should be cleaned up with a round file before reassembly.

2) Rear Suspension

a) Squeak – In the case of rear suspension appearing to squeak the problem is often caused by slackness of the adjustable foot of the thin carrier strut found on 'Series One' and earlier 'Series Two' Moultons. The foot of this strut can be tightened by removing the two self-tapping screws which hold it onto the main beam adjacent to the rear suspension rubber. The stay may then be swung forward and the foot rotated on its screw thread to take up the slack then swung back into position and screwed down. Avoid over-tightening as the very slight flexing of the frame under extreme load conditions can cause the adjuster thread to strip, (e.g. if the machine is ridden over very rough terrain at speed with a heavy rider and heavily laden rear carrier).

Another possible cause of rear suspension squeak is more serious and is often found in neglected machines which have been left out in the rain for prolonged periods; the pivot bolt rusts solid with its steel sleeving.

In time this leads to excessive wear of the pivot holes in the forks accompanied by a tendency for the rear wheel to wobble sideways slightly (e.g. when cornering). As a visual check, remember that the pivot nuts should move with the rear forks – get someone heavy to sit on the stationary bike and bounce whilst you watch the pivot nuts very carefully. (It is not as easy as you might think because the movement at the pivot is very slight).

If the pivot bolt has rusted in, first obtain a new bolt, sleeve and nylon bushes. It is then advisable to remove the rear wheel, mudguard and brake and disconnect the cables and chain. If the machine in question is a 'Mk III', remove the rear carrier and strut.

Next, it will almost certainly be necessary to saw through the old bolt on both sides of the machine. Ensure that your hacksaw blade goes through the lip of the nylon bush and does not damage the fork or the main frame. If your machine is one of the earlier ones with phosphor-bronze bushes, the job will be considerably harder.

When you have sawn through both sides (assuming that the bicycle is a 'Series One' or 'Two') unscrew the Phillips screws which hold the rubber suspension medium and its steel surround to the end of the main beam of the frame. The rear fork can now be removed. If the machine is a 'Mk III' release the 'squashball' retaining bolt before removing the rear triangle.

It is now necessary to punch out the pivot bolt, sleeve and what remains of the nylon bushes. In extreme cases this can be very awkward and time consuming, and it may be necessary to drill out the redundant parts. Plus Gas, LPS 1 or penetrating oil may help but do not forget to thoroughly wipe away any oil based products before reassembling the suspension.

Reassembly is much easier. Tap in the nylon bushes and gently tap in the pivot sleeve, ensuring that neither end protrudes beyond the faces of the bushes. Grease the pivot bolt well (you will not want to repeat the operation in a hurry!). Reposition the rear forks and pass the pivot bolt through the forks and the pivot sleeve, then fit the castellated washers and nuts, ensuring that the bolt protrudes by an equal margin either side of the forks. Finally replace the Phillips screws or 'squashball' bolt.

b) **Cracking** – Certain rear suspension units on 'Series One' machines, particularly those made at Kirkby during the changeover to CO_2 welding, are prone to developing hairline cracks on the underside of the rear forks adjacent to the base plate. Most defective units will have been discovered years ago no doubt but the problem is worth bearing in mind particularly if you are purchasing an old machine. The best remedy is replacement, preferably with 'Series Two' rear forks. These are in very short supply though, and Moulton Preservation can advise on ways of having the 'Series One' forks satisfactorily repaired. On no account should you discard any Moulton rear forks.

Cracking can also occur where the pivot tube passes through the main beam. This is generally less serious and a frame builder should be able to repair the damage. However, make sure that the suspension unit is removed first including the nylon bushes.

If the pivot bolt has not rusted to its sleeve, removal of the rear suspension is much easier. First, remove the rear wheel, brake and mudguard, then unscrew the three Phillips screws which hold the rubber suspension medium and its steel surround to the end of the main beam. (two in the top, one underneath). Then unscrew one pivot nut and gently tap out the pivot bolt. It is important to ensure that the bolt thread does not become distorted during this process. The rear forks may now be detached.

Reverse the procedure to reassemble, ensuring that the pivot bolt is well greased and that it protrudes by an equal amount either side of the forks.

c) **Twisting** – Some 'Series One' rear forks were also liable to twist under the torque created by frequent starting up under load (e.g. when the bicycle was used for door to door deliveries). The result was that the right-hand fork was pulled into a higher position than its opposite number. Consequently the rear wheel ran slightly out of vertical, when viewed from behind. Sometimes, with care, the forks arms can be levered back into alignment but this may further weaken the unit and the best remedy is replacement with 'Series Two' forks where possible.

3) Seat Tube Sag

Another point to bear in mind if buying second-hand is that, if ridden very hard under load, particularly with the seat pillar fully extended, the seat tube may in certain cases settle back very slightly, thus resulting in a shallower tube angle. Total seat tube failure is rare unless the machine has been grossly abused (e.g. by carrying an adult passenger on the rear carrier).

4) Back Wheel Clatter

Those who ride Moultons with hub gears and 1 3/8" tyres pumped up much higher than the recommended pressures, say to 80 p.s.i. will probably experience a rattling when free-wheeling over slightly pitted surfaces. This also happens with the 1¼" high pressure tyres. No amount of hub adjustment seems to solve the problem and it appears to be caused by the pawls of the free-wheel assembly momentarily engaging and disengaging as the rear suspension rides over the pitted surface. I know of no cure other than to reduce tyre pressure, which rather defeats the object. Many Moulton enthusiasts appear never to have experienced the problem although I have suffered it with all four of my machines.

Jack Lauterwasser, a leading authority on hub gears, has spent a considerable time investigating this problem but has been unable to produce a solution. My advice is to ignore the rattle as it is quite harmless.

5) Seat Tube Quick Release Problems

The original toggle, though more convenient to 'park' than some other maker's designs, has a tendency to snap near its pivoted end. If a genuine part is unobtainable a rival manufacturers' component will usually fit or a conventional spanner adjusted bolt may be substituted. The toggle used on the Dawes 'Kingpin' is very similar to the Moulton type.

6) 14" Wheel Versions Without Front Suspension

These machines, made by Raleigh, are subject to the possibility of cracking of the frame around the junction of the main beam and head tube. A reinforcing plate is available from Raleigh and this is easily fitted without special tools.

7) 14" Wheel Versions – Rear Carrier Sag

If grossly overloaded (e.g. by carrying a passenger), these rear carriers tend to sag, the carrier beam bending sharply immediately behind its junction with the thin strut and tie. Sometimes the carrier can still be used thereafter, providing that you do not mind it sloping down at about 20° to the horizontal. In other cases it may be advisable to braze up the bend in the carrier beam. The strongest solution would be to completely detach the carrier and braze it back into its original position, using a steel liner in the carrier beam to maintain alignment and strengthen the joint.

8) Stowaway Main Beam Joints

See Note 4) Chapter 7 and Appendix B) 10.

G) USEFUL TIPS

i) When was Your Moulton Made? This is easily determined with most machines made before the Raleigh takeover. On the left hand side of the seat tube, right at the top, you will find a letter and two numbers (e.g. B63 denotes a machine made at Bradford-on-Avon in 1963 whereas K65 shows the bike was made at Kirkby in 1965).

On the right hand side of the seat tube, also at the top, is a series of numbers. The first two show the week of the year. The remainder being the production number for that week. (e.g. 02758 would be the 758th machine made in the second week of January).

Unfortunately, the Raleigh numbering system does not seem to follow any readily discernible logic with regards to production dates. On 'Mk III's' the frame number is on the rear fork drop-out.

ii) Rubber Bellows Torn? If you are unable to obtain the correct Moulton front suspension bellows remember that similar items are found all over most motor cars (e.g. on gear lever and steering linkages). Try your local garage or spare parts dealer and ask to see a selection of 'boots' or 'gaiters'.

It may be necessary to perform a little deft surgery with a sharp Stanley knife in order to get a good fitting at the top and bottom but this is preferable to getting grit on the suspension splines.

iii) Front Suspension Too Soft? Assuming that the rubber column, compression spring, abutment and other parts are all present and correct, you can easily uprate the suspension by removing the abutment (see Appendix F) 1) Front Suspension), inserting washers of the same diameter as the abutment and then reinstating the abutment. The more washers you add, the harder the suspension will become. Try about 1/3" depth of washers initially.

With a second-hand machine the suspension may be soft because someone has removed the abutment. If you cannot obtain a replacement it should be possible to improvise a solution (e.g. an abutment could be fabricated out of hardwood dowelling to match the internal diameter of the steering column. The abutment should be ½ – ¾" long if it is to rest on top of the brake bolt).

iv) Front Suspension Brake Bush Missing? If there is no brake bush but the brake bolt holes in the abutment and fork crown are substantially larger than the brake bolt diameter, this indicates a missing brake bush. A replacement can be cut from ¼" steel motor car brake line tubing – beg an off-cut from your local garage!

v) 'Mk III' Rear Suspension Too Soft? This will usually apply only if you want to ride very hard and fast. Additional damping can be added by encircling the 'squashball' with a large jubilee clip. The tighter the clip screw is wound, the greater the damping. This method is used by David Duffield on one of his Moultons.

vi) Want to Fit a Front Carrier or Basket? The original frame-fixed front carriers are very scarce but the current version of the Raleigh '20 Shopper' has a somewhat similar carrier which might be adaptable for use with the brazed-on fittings on 'Series One and Two' Moultons.

Plastic-covered wire baskets are readily available from cycle shops and I have seen one of these successfully fitted to a Moulton head tube by means of jubilee clips.

It is not advisable to fix a basket or bag of any great size to the handlebars because the very light steering may be adversely affected.

vii) Got Minor Dents in the Frame? Try Holts Knifing Compound as used for similar defects in motor car bodywork.

viii) Frame (and Feet?) Getting Too Muddy in the Wet? The tangential spray angle from the small wheels is greater than on a big-wheeled bike and hence mudflaps are recommended. If you ride in company fit them to both mudguards.

ix) Problems with the 'Long' Type Prop Stand? The fixing clip of this stand has a nasty tendency to skew round thus 'chewing' the cross-bar and damaging the paintwork.

Make good the damage, ensure that the clip is correctly positioned and then drill a small hole through the right-hand side of the clip, into the cross-bar. Fix a small self-tapping screw through the clip into the cross-bar and this should prevent the problem recurring.

x) **Fed up with 10" Pumps?** The small inflators fitted to most 'Series One/Two' machines do not encourage the high tyre pressures required for the Moulton but a 17" pump can easily be fitted. Simply saw the front pump peg off the carrier and fix a 'Cyclo' pump peg to the carrier beam about 7" nearer the front of the bike. The very first production Moultons used this method of pump fixing.

It is well worth buying a small brass Schrader valve adaptor which will enable you to inflate your Moulton tyres with a foot-operated motor car pump — a much easier operation!

xi) Frightened of a Front Wheel Puncture? It has been suggested that a fast front wheel puncture at high speed can be more dangerous on a small-wheeled bicycle than on a conventional machine.

If this worries you ensure that your front tyre is free from defects and has a good depth of tread. Also, make certain that the inner tube and rim tape are in good condition, and that the cover beads are correctly seated. Tyre savers or flint catchers are light but useful accessories. If you adopt these precautions you are unlikely to run into trouble.

If you are *particularly* worried about punctures you could try the new 'Mr. Tuffy' tape which is a plastic material fitted between the cover and the inner tube. It is certainly very effective at preventing thorns and flints from piercing the inner tube but I would expect it to have some slight detrimental effects on the performance and handling of the 1¼" Moulton tyre.

xii) Thinking of Fitting 17 x 1¼" Wheels? Remember that you will almost certainly need a new front brake because the steel stirrup fitted to most 16" wheel Moultons does not permit the brake blocks to be positioned high enough to operate on the 17" wheels.

If you decide to buy a new pair of brakes remember that a stirrup pattern suitable for 17" use at the front may offer a very limited adjustment range for your 17" rear wheel. It is advisable to check the dimensions carefully before purchasing.

xiii) Dynohub Bulbs? A hub dynamo rotates much faster in a Moulton wheel than in a conventional wheel for a given road speed. It will produce enough power to cast a headlamp beam even at walking pace. Consequently, if you use bulbs intended for conventional machines you may find that they tend to burn out prematurely.

The U.K. regulations concerning bicycle lighting have been toughened in recent years and if you experience problems with Dynohub-fed bulbs blowing, it is advisable to contact the manufacturers (Sturmey-Archer) for their latest recommendations.

Moulton bicycle Dynohub lamps were originally fitted with a 6V. 0.25 A bulb at the front and a 6V. 0.1A bulb at the rear.

There is no parallel problem with tyre driven dynamos because their output is unaffected by wheel size.

xiv) Cable Guides Missing? If you do not wish to have new guides brazed on and do not want the bicycle to be covered in strips of insulating tape, drill small holes in the required guide positions and 'Araldite' in suitably sized metal eyes (as sold in hardware stores for curtain rails etc.). These can then be painted to the frame colour if so desired.

H) SPARES

This is very much a case of every man for himself. Mike Woolf at Moulton Preservation can give useful guidance and Alex Moulton Limited have a very limited supply of certain spares. Be prepared to keep knocking at the doors of cycle dealers. When it comes to queries concerning the Moulton, letters frequently go unanswered even by the most famous and reputable firms. If an answer is received it is often negative even when it is well-known that the dealer has the parts. It is easier to say no, than 'waste time' looking around or asking members of staff. It is even easier to 'lose the letter'.

Often you will get different answers from different sales people in the same shop, or even from the same person at different times, depending on the 'stress factor'. Bear in mind that younger staff may not even know what a Moulton is while others may think it is a generic term for small-wheeled bicycles. Also, remember that many dealers, especially frame builders of the old school, tend to be openly hostile to the Moulton and on mention of the name you should be prepared to receive a sermon laced with all sorts of mythology about what a disaster the Moulton was (and it's no good pointing out that the only reason he is still in business is the small-wheel market created by the Moulton!). Nonetheless, persistence pays and it is amazing how enthusiastic some people in the trade can be. I recently heard of a wholesaler who personally delivered two 16 x 1 3/8" ribbed tyres, deliberately 'salted away' six years before, just so that he could see a Moulton undergoing restoration!

As the spares situation is constantly changing and as this book may be in circulation for some time, it would be unwise to give too much specific information on spares availability. However in late 1981 it was still possible of obtain complete unused front suspension units from several sources. Certain types of mudguard and the standard 52 tooth chainwheel were also readily available. Rear suspension pivot assemblies were scarce but the situation looked likely to improve.

Replacement rear forks for 'Series One/Two' machines were very scarce but a new method of refurbishing defective units had recently been evolved. The carrier and holdall situation, though fairly bleak, looked likely to improve (one of Midland's rear holdalls, at about £6.40 in 1981, will serve adequately for utility purposes, being fairly close to the original Moulton holdall size and shape).

If you do experience genuine difficulty in obtaining spares which are exclusive to the Moulton, the best advice is to contact Moulton Preservation who will update you on the latest position. Conversely, if you find a hidden cache of Moulton parts, please let them know. Please remember that Moulton Preservation is a non-profit-making voluntary organisation.

I) USEFUL ADDRESSES

1) MOULTON BICYCLE CLUB
   Website: www.moultoneers.info

2) MOULTON PRESERVATION
   Michael Woolf
   21 Cremorne Road
   World's End
   Chelsea
   LONDON
   SW10 0NB

3) MOULTON BICYCLE COMPANY
   Holt Road
   BRADFORD-ON-AVON
   Wiltshire
   BA15 1AH
   Email: office@moultonbicycles.co.uk
   Website: www.moultonbicycles.co.uk

4) TONY HADLAND
   4 Barcote Cottages
   Buckland
   FARINGDON
   Oxfordshire
   SN7 8PP
   Email: tony.hadland@gmail.com or tony@hadland.net
   Website: hadland.wordpress.com or hadland.net

ADDITIONAL INFORMATION AND CORRECTIONS

Page 25, picture caption: For 'John Emery' read 'Roger Norman'

Page 26, Note 3: This cycle was called 'Le Petit Bi' and was designed in 1938 by a Frenchman, A. J. Marcelin. In common with many other cycling developments of the time (such as the Sturmey-Archer five-speed gear) it was overshadowed by the war; indeed, Alex Moulton only became aware of its existence when Tony Hadland drew it to his attention. For more on 'Le Petit Bi', visit hadland.wordpress.com

Page 45, Note 1: After working for many major bicycle makers and as a sports commentator on TV, David Duffield is now retired.

Page 46, Note 5: Raleigh no longer provide this bracket.

Page 55, first para: The AM series of Moulton bicycles was launched on 19th May 1983. See *The Spaceframe Moultons* by Tony Hadland.

Page 76, Note 1, second para. Alan Lauterwasser no longer works for Peugeot cycles.

Page 79, penultimate line: The Gian Robert item was merely the derailleur mechanism, not the sprocket cluster.

Page 108, Export Models: Moultons were assembled and marketed under licence in Australia by Electronics Industries Limited, under their Malvern Star trade mark. Also, the design was pirated by the Communist Chinese, who produced a Moulton copy at Shanghai under the Phoenix trade mark. This had a frame somewhat similar to that of the 7/8th scale Moulton but used 16" wheels. For more on export and licence-built Moultons, see *'Classic' Moultons Abroad* by Paul Grogan.

Page 122: In 1984 Dr. Chester Kyle of the International Human Powered Vehicle Association tested the Moulton 17" tyres at pressures of 90 and 120 psi. The results were comparable with those from a cotton road tubular (sewup) tyre or a high quality 27" High Pressure touring tyre.

Page 131 iv): These tubular tyres are no longer available except handmade to special order.

Page 136 viii): An FW can be converted into an S52 by fitting a complete S52 axle assembly in place of the comparable FW parts. This is a relatively easy operation.

Page 137: Cyclo no longer produce derailleur converters. The Rogers unit is no longer available and was welded, not brazed. Both SRAM and Sturmey-Archer produce 3speed hub gears combined with multiple sprockets.

Page 147, Appendix G i): Michael Woolf of Moulton Preservation has made a study of the frame numbering system and has never encountered a B prefix. Bradford made bikes are recognisable by pop-riveting, good workmanship, and, in some cases, an extra long number incorporating the year of manufacture, e.g. 64100009 being an actual Stowaway made at Bradford-on-Avon in 1964.

Not all Kirkby-produced machines received the K prefix, though most did. To onfuse the issue further, sometimes the year number is on the right of the seat tube top with the serial number on the left. Generally, the serial number consisted of six digits, the first two being the week of the year, the rest being the number in that week's batch. Sometimes shorter numbers are found and one of the author's bikes had no week prefix (K65 250). At one stage, deliberately misleading numbers were used to confuse Raleigh's marketing people.

If you cannot find a serial number in the usual places, look at the underside of the bottom bracket shell.

As stated in the book, Raleigh numbers follow no easily discernible convention. Generally they are of 6 or 7 digits and commence with 0.

For more information, see *The 'Classic' Moulton* by Paul Grogan.

Bicycle Science

Tony Hadland
The Spaceframe Moultons
"Re-reading today Tony Hadland's book "The Spaceframe Moultons" brings back what a splendid job he did in researching and describing those exciting events which led up to the birth of the Spaceframe Moulton."
Alex Moulton
2009, 384 S., 59,90 €, gb., ISBN 978-3-643-10357-4